# NARRATIVE AND ARGUMENT

**Open University Press**

English, Language, and Education series

*General Editor:* Anthony Adams

Lecturer in Education, University of Cambridge

This series is concerned with all aspects of language in education
from the primary school to the tertiary sector. Its authors are
experienced educators who examine both principles and practice of
English subject teaching and language across the curriculum in the
context of current educational and societal developments.

## TITLES IN THE SERIES

**Narrative and Argument**
Richard Andrews (ed.)

**Time for Drama**
Roma Burgess and Pamela Gaudry

**Computers and Literacy**
Daniel Chandler and Stephen Marcus (eds)

**Readers, Texts, Teachers**
Bill Corcoran and Emrys Evans (eds)

**Developing Response to Poetry**
Patrick Dias and Michael Hayhoe

**The Primary Language Book**
Peter Dougill and Richard Knott

**Children Talk About Books: Seeing
Themselves as Readers**
Donald Fry

**Literary Theory and English Teaching**
Peter Griffith

**Assessing English**
Brian Johnston

**Lipservice: The Story of Talk in Schools**
Pat Jones

**The English Department in a
Changing World**
Richard Knott

**Oracy Matters**
Margaret MacLure, Terry Phillips and
Andrew Wilkinson (eds)

**Teaching Literature for Examinations**
Robert Protherough

**Developing Response to Fiction**
Robert Protherough

**Microcomputers and the Language Arts**
Brent Robinson

**English Teaching from A–Z**
Wayne Sawyer, Anthony Adams and
Ken Watson

**Collaboration and Writing**
Morag Styles (ed.)

**Reconstructing 'A' Level English**
Patrick Scott

**English Teaching in Perspective**
Ken Watson

**The Quality of Writing**
Andrew Wilkinson

**The Writing of Writing**
Andrew Wilkinson (ed.)

# NARRATIVE AND ARGUMENT

EDITED BY ·
**Richard Andrews**

Open University Press
*Milton Keynes · Philadelphia*

Open University Press
12 Cofferidge Close
Stony Stratford
Milton Keynes MK11 1BY

and
1900 Frost Road, Suite 101
Bristol, PA 19007, USA

First Published 1989

**British Library Cataloguing in Publication Data**
Narrative and argument.—(English, language, and
    education series)
　1. English language rhetoric
　Andrews, Richard　　II. Series
　808′42
　ISBN 0-335-09219-5 (paper)

**Library of Congress Cataloging-in-Publication Data**
Narrative and argument / edited by Richard Andrews.
　　　　p.　　cm.—(English, language, and education)
　Bibliography: p.
　Includes index.
　ISBN 0-335-09219-5
　1. English language—Composition and exercises—Study and
teaching.　2. English language—Rhetoric—Study and teaching.
3. Narration (Rhetoric)　4. Persuasion (Rhetoric)　I. Andrews,
Richard, 1953– .　II. Series.
PE1404.N37　1989
808′.042′07—dc20　　　　　　　　　　　　　　　　89–32389
　　　　　　　　　　　　　　　　　　　　　　　　　　　　　CIP

**349676**

Typeset by Rowland Phototypesetting Limited
Bury St Edmunds, Suffolk
Printed in Great Britain by Biddles Limited
Guildford and King's Lynn

# Contents

# List of contributors

*Gunther Kress* teaches in the Communication programmes at the University of Technology, Sydney. He is a member of the Literacy and Education Research Network (LERN). Among his books are *Learning to Write*, *Linguistic Processes in Sociocultural Practice*, *Social Semiotics* (with R. Hodge) and the forthcoming *Writing as Social Practice*.

*Peter Medway* is Senior Research Fellow in the University of Leeds, working on the Technical and Vocational Education Initiative (TVEI). He has taught English in various comprehensive schools and has lectured widely in Britain, North America and Australia. He is author of *Finding a Language* and co-author with Mike Torbe of *The Climate for Learning*.

*Carol Fox's* special interest is in the ways children may become literate before the acquisition of independent reading and writing, and she has studied this through their invented oral stories. She is Senior Lecturer in the Faculty of Education at Brighton Polytechnic.

*Brian Cambourne* is Head of the Centre for Studies in Literacy at the University of Wollongong, Australia. He works within a naturalistic paradigm of inquiry, using a 'teacher-as-co-researcher' model of collaborative research with practising teachers.

*Hazel Brown* is a primary school teacher in New South Wales, and has been co-researcher with Brian Cambourne during the last four years. Together they have been trying to develop a grounded theory of literacy education and have published several books and papers on their findings.

*Ian Frowe* read philosophy at the Universities of Wales, Exeter and Liverpool. At present he is a primary school teacher on Merseyside.

*Roslyn Arnold* is Senior Lecturer in Education (English/Drama) at the University of Sydney. She has researched the development of writing abilities and is now interested in the relationship between self-psychology and language development.

*Aviva Freedman* is Head of the Department of Linguistics at Carleton University, Ottawa. She has co-authored a number of studies of writing development and the evaluation of writing for the Ontario Ministry of Education, and has published many articles on writing development at both school and university level.

*Ian Pringle* is an Associate Professor of Linguistics and English at Carleton University, Ottawa, and Director of the Centre for Applied Language Studies there. He has collaborated with Aviva Freedman on a number of studies of writing development, and is co-editor with her of *Reinventing the Rhetorical Tradition, Teaching Writing Learning, Learning to Write: First Language, Second Language* and of a number of research studies and articles.

*Stephen Clarke* is Lecturer in Education at the University of Leeds, and is currently researching English teachers starting work. He is co-author, with Douglas and Dorothy Barnes, of *Versions of English*.

*John Sinker* was, until recently, Head of English in a comprehensive school in Leeds, and has pursued questions of education administration as well as matters concerning English. He is at present an advisory teacher for the Leeds Education Authority.

*Judith Atkinson* is Head of English at Wolfreton School, Hull. She has taught in five secondary schools, and is an active member of the National Association of Teachers of English. She has contributed articles and essays to several publications and is co-author of *The Effective Teaching of English*.

*Douglas Hesse* is Director of Writing Programs and Assistant Professor of English at Illinois State University. He has published chapters in *Literary Nonfiction, Essays on the Essay* and *Where is Short Story Criticism?*

*John Dixon* has recently been reconsidering *Writing Narrative – and Beyond* with Leslie Stratta and *Levels of Abstracting* (including narrative) with Aviva Freedman. His contribution is part of a longer-term enquiry into the (often untheorized) options adopted in literary critical discourse since English Literature became institutionalized in the universities.

# Acknowledgements

This book had its beginnings in conversations with Andy Homden (historian) and Richard Dyer (mathematician) as part of a small research project initiated by Island School, Hong Kong, in 1987. I am grateful to them, and to the rest of the staff at the school, for their co-operation.

There is a more long-standing debt to be honoured to Geoffrey Summerfield for his inspiration, to Fred Manley for his storytelling at George Green's School on London's Isle of Dogs, and to Michael Simons and Harold Rosen for their interest and encouragement.

Finally, I would like to thank Anthony Adams for his enthusiasm and fine judgement, the contributors for their insight and efficiency, and John Skelton at Open University Press for his support during the making of the book.

# List of abbreviations and terms

| | |
|---|---|
| CSE | Certificate of Secondary Education, the less academic counterpart of GCE in examinations at sixteen plus in England and Wales until the mid-eighties |
| DARTS | Directed Activities Relating to Texts |
| DES | Department of Education and Science |
| GCE | General Certificate in Education which, at sixteen plus, preceded GCSE |
| GCSE | General Certificate of Secondary Education |
| Grammar school | The academic part of the hierarchical system of state education 11–18 which preceded comprehensive schooling in England and Wales |
| HSC | Higher School Certificate, the final school leaving examination in Australia |
| JMB | Joint Matriculation Board, one of the examination boards incorporated within the five new examination boards in England and Wales |
| NEA | Northern Examining Association, one of the five examination boards in England and Wales |
| PGCE | Postgraduate Certificate in Education, a one-year university training course for intending graduate teachers |
| TVEI | Technical and Vocational Education Initiative |

*Note*
In general, in England and Wales, infant classes correspond to Grades 1 and 2 in North America and Years 1 and 2 in Australia; junior classes to Grades and Years 3 to 6; secondary classes (termed 1st Year at 11/12 through to 6th year at 16/18) to Grades and Years 7 to 13. There is currently a government proposal to describe the years of schooling in England and Wales along the lines of Australian practice (Years 1–13).

# General editor's introduction

Richard Andrews may be best known so far to readers of this book as someone who has collaborated with Geoffrey Summerfield in the production of unusually successful materials for the classroom English teacher. He has recently been appointed to the School of Education at the University of Hull.

The present volume represents a new departure for him, and, possibly, for this series. It is, like Peter Griffith's *Literary Theory and English Teaching*, rather more theoretical in its stance than most of the books we have published; nevertheless, we expect it to be both accessible and helpful to the classroom teacher of English, particularly at secondary level.

In his own introduction Richard begins with some references to the work of Freedman and Pringle in Canada, and it was their work and a conference they organized at Carleton University, leading to the publication of *Reinventing the Rhetorical Tradition*, that first interested me in the field that is so ably surveyed here. The North American tradition of English teaching, in both universities and high schools, has been much more aware of 'rhetoric' than most recent work elsewhere and we have a good deal to learn from it.

Not the least virtue of the present volume is the range of international contributors of distinction that the editor has managed to assemble. I must confess that when the proposal was first made and the time-scale for the editing of the book was suggested, it seemed to me impossible to achieve so much in so short a space of time. It is one of Richard Andrews's great strengths as an editor that he has been able to weld together into a single coherent volume many experienced and distinguished writers in this way.

The coming of the General Certificate in Secondary Education in England and Wales has potentially opened up much wider areas of discourse than were generally to be found in the old Ordinary-level syllabuses. The insights provided here into a variety of genres within the general fields of narrative and argument should help teachers to open up new directions for their students so that they can be led to experiment more widely than has been traditional in secondary schools with the notion of form. The numerous examples from student work in several of the chapters show clearly how well they can write when freed from the tyranny of conventional (and limited) narrative structure.

This book is about writing; but it is also about thinking, and thinking about writing. If, in England and Wales, we are to make sense of the demands of writing within the national curriculum, the kind of thinking that is represented here becomes very necessary. We publish the book in the expectation that it will enable teachers of English to widen both the horizons and achievements of their students; we hope, too, that it will initiate a wider discussion of rhetoric within the British academic tradition.

*Anthony Adams*

# Introduction: new relationships between narrative and argument?

## RICHARD ANDREWS

There has been tremendous growth in the understanding of narrative in the last thirty years, and within the last ten years or so that interest has worked its way into schools. Storytelling, for instance, is alive and well, despite Walter Benjamin's fears: primary schools, in particular, have invited storytellers to perform and some secondary schools have encouraged telling and retelling not only in 'English' (and not only in the English language), but across the curriculum. Storytelling and story-writing are still the most dominant form in English lessons and in many ways this is to be celebrated. The question remains, however, as to the amount and quality of attention afforded other forms such as the essay, the speech and other less 'formal', more interactive forms that come under the heading of argument. There is still a general feeling that – up to age sixteen or so – students write better stories than arguments. Beyond sixteen, they are not given much chance to write anything but formal essays.

Attention to the nature, quality and extent of argument in education was given fresh impetus in the early 1980s by the work of Dixon and Stratta in England and of Freedman and Pringle in Canada. Dixon and Stratta (1982b) noted that 'argument within the English lesson seemed to be a very ill-defined area' and they suggested distinctions that might be made to begin to chart the kinds of argument attempted in schools: distinctions between personal argument and 'detached' debate; between arguments that lead to decision and action and those which are concerned with beliefs; between advocating and 'balanced' arguments; and between the ruminative essay and the essay which moves to a conclusion. Freedman and Pringle examined the relative success achieved by secondary school students in narrative and argumentative forms in a series of studies for the Carleton Board of Education (e.g. Freedman and Pringle 1979), and summarized some of their findings in Freedman and Pringle (1984).

The increasing interest in argument has been important, not only because it has helped teachers reflect on their practice in this area, but also because it is calling into question current assumptions about the relationship between argument and other modes of discourse. It is the particular relationships between narrative and argument on which I wish to focus in this introduction, and which are the principal focus of this book.

But why only narrative and argument? Why not include exposition, too? I was asked these questions by Peter Medway during the planning stages of this book, and they are good ones. In time, I found three answers. First, that of these three modes of discourse, exposition seems the least able to shape, transform and generate. Because its emphasis is on expositional clarity, there is not the same degree of importance attached to sequence as in narrative (where sequence is of the very nature of the mode) or in argument (where sequence is one of a range of rhetorical resources). Perhaps because its function is more referential than persuasive, it appears to be the most inert of the modes, borrowing structures from narrative or argument in order to give itself shape and direction. Second, exposition has all too often been conflated with argument and subsumed within it, and deserves separate consideration. Third, and following these first two points, a study of the relationships between exposition and the other two modes would be well worth further study, and would certainly require at least another book.

There is also a productive tension brought into play when narrative and argument are yoked together. Conventionally, narrative and argument are seen as belonging to separate worlds. Narrative, it is argued, is culturally and structurally less sophisticated than argument. It is dismissed in phrases like 'only a story' and 'anecdotal evidence', and associated primarily with childhood and fiction. Argument, on the other hand, is a 'high' cultural form, as evidenced by its use in government, in public debate, in academia and in business. It deals with outcomes in the 'real' world; it transacts and it embodies rationality and logic, the bases of science and of bureaucracy. Before we explore this relationship further, let us clarify terms.

Narrative (derived from the Latin *narro*, to relate or recount, and in turn from *gnarus*, knowing, and the Sanskrit *gnâ*, to know) is defined by Prince (1982) as 'the representation of at least two real or fictive events or situations in a time sequence, neither of which presupposes or entails the other'. Argument, as used in this book, has a more generalized nature than the specific dispute one might have with a colleague, partner and/or adversary. Although it has its roots there – as Frowe points out in Chapter 5 – there has been developed an entire network of checks and balances to temper the mode. Argument, then, might be provisionally defined as 'a connected series of statements or reasons intended to establish a position; a process of reasoning' (*OED*).

Still further, one needs to define the connections between such terms as 'mode', 'form', 'genre' and 'function' so that the level at which the argument (to use the word in another, but related sense) of this book proceeds might be determined. Sometimes it is hard to distinguish between function and mode, though – in the main – narrative and argument operate at the mode level. While the function of a discourse is its purpose within a social context, its mode is the vehicle it uses to effect that purpose. However, we cannot formulate the distinction between narrative and argument quite so neatly as to say argument = function and narrative = form or mode.

Once we have established the distinction between function and mode, definitions of 'genre' and 'form' can follow. Genres can be seen as cultural conventions at the modal level, and forms as subcategories of genre.[1] As Kress points out in Chapter 1, genre theory is not new, but presents a challenge to the discipline of 'English' as framed by '(late) Leavisite anti-mass culture romanticism [or] recent liberal individualist ideologies'.

It is clear that discussions of function and mode soon lead to the philosophical level. One particularly powerful notion that borders on this level is that even narrative literary discourse can be seen to have a social function. In his essay, Medway uses speech-act theory to argue the place for persuasiveness as the prime mover in social discourse. If we accept his case, a new light is shed upon the relationship between narrative and argument. If, for example, we take all discourses (including stories told 'for their own sake') to be in some degree persuasive (in that their function is to get things done, have effects or generate affects), then argument might be seen to hold the prime position in the relationship with narrative, because the argument of a narrative is concomitant with its function. In short, argument could be seen to operate at a level of generalization that is directly accessible from the narrative level (the level of particularities). It both informs by giving paradigmatic shape to a narrative, and is informed by the syntagmatic drive and direction of narrative. Or, in other words, there is a symbiotic relationship between narrative and argument.

What must be made clear at this point, however, is that breaking away from conventional beliefs about the relationship between narrative and argument (which in extreme form, hold that there is no relationship) does not mean that narrative and argument are to be seen as a single mode, or that narrative can be seen as the 'means' and argument as the 'end' of all discourse. It is necessary to preserve the distinction between them. They are different at the modal level in that, in the words of Kress, argument

> provides . . . the means for bringing difference into existence. At the same time, it provides conventionalized textual forms not just for maintaining and tolerating difference, but for culturally productive use of difference . . . Narrative, as a textual form, provides means of resolution of difference . . .

Here, then, is the territory that this book seeks to explore. Rather than viewing narrative and argument as opposite poles of the rhetorical world, is it possible that their relationship is less one of polarity and mutual suspicion than of generative interdependence? Rather than narrative appearing as a mere element in the arrangement of an argument (as Aristotle's *Rhetorica* would have it), or, on the other hand, narrative being the centre piece of a theory of discourse, mind and cultural form (as the narratologists would have it), might the classical tradition be combined with narrative theory and practice to produce a theory of discourse that empowers writers of all kinds (from learner-writers to professional novelists, from producers of advertising copy to writers of company reports) by giving them not only a link between the 'naturally' acquired narrative competences and the demands of persuasive (and expositional) discourse, but also a choice of strategies available at the 'point of utterance'?

It is the attempt to bridge the gap between theories of discourse and the practice of learning to write (and the best teaching methods to employ to help that learning) that underpins this volume, because it seems to me that there is a dangerous chasm between, say, the theory outlined in Kinneavy (1971) and Kinneavy *et al.* (1985), on the one hand, and the work of Graves (1983) and the 'process' movement, on the other. One is virtually all theory, and the attempt to apply it to the classroom makes for dry 'textbook' material; the other celebrates process to such a degree that insufficient perspective is gained to enable the learner-writer to develop command of the forms offered by the social and cultural nexus.

This dualistic gap – between theory and practice, science and the arts, argument and narrative – reinforced by the conflation of exposition and argument, is reaffirmed by Bruner (1986), who quotes William James for his epigraph:

> To say that all human thinking is essentially of two kinds – reasoning on the one hand, and narrative, descriptive, contemplative thinking on the other – is to say only what every reader's experience will corroborate.

And so the argument continues until 'In the end . . . the narrative and the paradigmatic come to live side by side' (Bruner 1986, p. 43). That seems to be a conservative conclusion to what could have been a breakthrough in our understanding of the relationship between the two modes, but after these tantalizing foundational chapters, Bruner moves on into the psycho-cultural area. Rosen (1988b) questions Bruner's formulation in what he calls a 'flawed' chapter; Bruner's weakness is seen as his narrow conception of what constitutes narrative for the purposes of his argument, in that he concentrates only on the literary kind.

What is at stake here is more than the result of an intellectual debate. Practice in the teaching of writing at pre-school, primary, secondary and tertiary level is everything to do with the theory that informs it, and it seems to me that the various countries and traditions that have explored practice both to and from high levels of abstraction have a great deal to offer each other. In particular, North American traditions in rhetoric, British practice in expressive writing and in story formation, and Australian debate about genre and register need to be brought closer together and to share a common language. Work in the theory of discourse in other countries, too, needs to be brought into the fold.

It is to these ends that the central section of this collection runs chronologically from Carol Fox's essay (Chapter 3) on the told stories of a five-year-old to Douglas Hesse's consideration (Chapter 10) of the college essay in the light of what we could call 'neo-Aristotelian' theory.

Fox argues that, far from the commonly held notion that children cannot argue until they have acquired what Piaget calls 'formal operations', argument is present in the narratives of young children in largely implicit form. As Moffett (1968) suggested, for children for a long time, 'narrative must do for all', but that does not mean to say that narrative is the only (limited) kind of message that can be conveyed. The presence of narrative gives shape to as well as enriches and enlivens the arguments. It can be said here, too, that conventional assumptions about the developmental relationship between narrative and argument (conventions embodied in proposed attainment targets in writing, see DES 1988) not only see narrative as preceding argument, but as purely 'chronological' writing.[2]

In Chapter 4, Cambourne and Brown present a 'grounded theory' of the acquisition of different registers, based on the teaching of Hazel Brown in a primary school in New South Wales. They suggest that children of this age can learn to control various registers if they are supported within a classroom environment that provides them with the necessary models (largely in the form of reading material), contexts and attention. 'Register' as used here is almost like 'mode' or 'genre'. It is a term which allows greater commerce between the levels of function and mode in that it is taken to refer to 'types of . . . discourse . . . which serve specific functions [or which] have specific organizational characteristics'. The social determinants of choice of mode are thus made more accessible, while the taxonomy of types – a taxonomy that sees 'exposition' as a register that is synonymous with argument – delimits the field.

Frowe's essay (Chapter 5) is also based on classroom practice, and gives an account of his work with primary school children in the basics of formal arguing that are rarely seen at this level, and yet which seem both enjoyable and convincing. It is well worth comparing his principles and practice with the exemplary community of enquiry created in Hardcastle's classroom, as mentioned by Medway (Chapter 2).

Moving on (and, by the way, this is a chronological arrangement despite the 'non-chronological' expositional nature of this part of the introduction), Arnold (Chapter 6) reflects on a study she made of longitudinal development in the acquisition of rhetorical competence, and argues for our attention as teachers to be directed more to what the children want to say than to the forms in which we might want them to write; as such, she provides us with a salutary reminder of the purpose of a book like this.

Freedman and Pringle, in a retrospective essay (Chapter 7) based on research in schools that spans some ten years, look in particular at the way argument is approached and at the reasons for the relative lack of competence in the writing of argument in schoolchildren compared to their facility in the composition of narratives. They refer to the pioneering work of Dixon and Stratta mentioned earlier in this introduction, and to their own earlier essay which appeared in *English in Education* in 1984, alongside an article by Stephen Clarke, 'An Area of Neglect'.

Clarke's interest in this neglected area of the teaching of argument is extended in his and Sinker's piece (Chapter 8) on travel writing, which aims to explore the possibilities of developing rationalization 'through the anecdotal form of auto-biographical narrative'. What is so appropriate about travel writing in particular for this purpose is that, going beyond the autobiographical impetus, it takes young writers to a point of entry into discourses which are disparate yet may have continuous application in making meaning through argument.

One particular external constraint on the way children shape their writing as they move through secondary school is, of course, the form of assessment at the end of the course. In Chapter 9, Atkinson looks at the way argument is examined in the relatively recent GCSE syllabuses, and puts this in the context of past practices and papers. From that point, we leap to college composition with Hesse's piece (Chapter 10) on the nature of the essay and on narrative's increasing colonization of the territory previously held to be the province of argument. And so, from 'Divine Dialogues' to 'Persuading as Storying' we move full circle: from pre-school to college, from story-as-argument to argument-as-story.

The collection is concluded, and perhaps given new direction, in John Dixon's review article (Chapter 11) of a recent book by Imre Salusinszky (1987) in which the author discusses a Wallace Stevens poem with various eminent critics. In the essay, Dixon moves the focus of the present volume beyond writing and speech to reading, applying the distinction between narrative and argument to his reading of both the poem and the critical positions, and at the same time couching his response in both narrative and argumentative form.

Dixon's essay is a fitting end to this volume, for the principle of marrying theory and practice has been an aim throughout. What *Narrative and Argument* tries to do is to question existing assumptions about the relationship of the two modes of discourse, to suggest ways in which progress might be made in this area, and to move towards a new rhetoric in which 'shaping at the point of utterance' is informed by a range of possible rhetorical choices. In this way, it is hoped that children in our schools and students in schools and colleges will be able to draw on the liveliness and shapeliness of their existing discourse competences in order to take command of kinds of discourse which might previously have been beyond their reach; to argue more competently and more powerfully; and perhaps to generate new kinds of discourse.

## Notes

1 Terms used in schools and colleges to describe the forms employed in writing are not without confusion and controversy. Many teachers still use 'essay' to cover any piece of continuous writing (including stories), whereas others see 'essay' as a more specific form of argument and as one kind of composition. 'Composition', though currently out of favour in Britain, is perhaps the most useful general term; 'creative writing' blurs the distinction between the various forms it takes. While these points are only of marginal interest in themselves, they do suggest the (unconscious) thinking behind the use of such terms, and are of crucial importance to the students who have to do the writing.

2 No one who has read Fitzgerald, Ricoeur (1984; 1985; 1988) or *The Beano* could maintain that all narrative writing is chronological, any more than all 'non-narrative writing' is 'non-chronological'.

# 1 Texture and meaning

GUNTHER KRESS

## Genre

The category of genre is not new: it has a history that goes back to Aristotle's *Poetics* at least. From this venerable history in Western literary traditions it has emerged, over the last two or three decades, in the broad area of popular culture (for instance in film theory, in popular fiction, in television study) and in ethnographics of language. This has proved a decisive point in turning the study of genre from the field of high culture, with its formal and aesthetic interests, towards the social, the popular, towards broadly political concerns. Most recently there has been a vigorous interest in the area of genre in education – in work on literacy (Kress 1982; Martin and Rothery 1981b; Painter and Martin 1986) and on broader applications in curriculum theory (Christie 1985a; 1985b); this work shares similar social and political aims. Yet while the use of the category of genre proved entirely unproblematic in popular culture as in sociolinguistics – after all, no-one has worried about the use of labels such as 'Musical', 'Western', 'roadmovie', 'film noir', 'romance', 'detective', 'Sci-Fi', 'fantasy', in relation to film or popular ('pulp'!) fiction – its use in education has proved highly contentious (Reid 1987).

The reasons for indifference in the one case and vigorous debate in the other, while highly complex, are not all that difficult to establish. Within education, in the discipline of English as in the broader domain of literacy, genre theory has proved to be a direct challenge to the established and entrenched hegemony of 'literature' in the form of high-cultural 'great' literature, as well as to a confluence of pedagogical views of a diverse and pervasive kind. The mix of these latter is, clearly, a different one from culture to culture, depending on particular histories. In Australia, in the 1980s, this mix included (late) Leavisite anti-mass culture romanticism, more recent liberal individualist ideologies – whether in the form of (late or neo-)Romantic notions of literature as the domain of individual creativity and expression, or of American West Coast individualist psychologisms. Romanticism – itself a reaction against the repressive authoritarianism of eighteenth-century European states – stressed the potential of the individual as creative, free, unfettered, heroic: the Promethean ideal. This heritage, long since the new orthodoxy, has been buttressed in the neo-Romantic movements of modernism (Joyce, Woolf) and post-modernism (Derrida). Within Romanticism as in the various neo-Romanticisms, genre defines that which is *not* literary: literature, in this tradition, is precisely that which 'escapes' the bounds of genre. (This argument is developed in more detail in Kress and Threadgold 1988.)

Genre theory in education is not, at this stage, a highly unified body of theory (Christie 1985a; 1985b; Kress 1982; 1985; 1988; Hodge and Kress 1988; Kress and Threadgold 1988; Martin 1984; 1985; Martin and Rothery 1981b; Reid 1987; Threadgold 1988a; 1988b; Threadgold *et al.* 1986). The contributors to this debate represent a significant range of distinctive positions. Nevertheless, genre theory operates with a broad set of shared assumptions. I list them here in point form, despite the fact that that mode of representation obscures the very real fluidity in that body of work. Genre theorists assume

1  that forms of text (genres) are the result of processes of social production;
2  that, given the relative stability of social structures, forms of text produced in and by specific social institutions, that is, the resultant genres, will attain a certain degree of stability and of persistence over time;
3  that consequently, texts in their generic form are not produced *ab initio* each time by an individual (or individuals) expressing an inner meaning, but are, rather, the effects of the action of individual social agents acting *both* within the bounds of their social history *and* the constraints of particular contexts, and with a knowledge of existing generic types;
4  that, given the social provenance of genres, different genres 'have', convey, and give access to different degrees and kinds of social power;
5  that genres have specifiable linguistic characteristics which are neither fully determined nor largely under the control of individual speakers or writers;
6  that knowledge of the characteristics of texts and of their social place and power can and should form a part of any curriculum, whether in one subject area, or 'across the curriculum'.

It will be obvious that this set of assumptions, despite significant divergences among genre theorists, nevertheless poses a fundamental challenge to the discipline of English as I described it above. It is, at one and the same time, quite out of step with the anti-structuralist stance of post-modernism, with its emphasis (in its linguistic/textual/literary manifestations) on the undecidability of meanings, the fluidity of texts, the infinite deferral of signification, the 'play of signifiers', the dispersed subject and, above all, the total rejection and therefore absence of anchorage in the social. Genre theory is consequently both entirely unfashionable – in its relation to post-modernism – and subversive of the established discipline of 'English' and its ideology of Romantic individualism.

From the point of view of both 'English' and of post-structuralism, genre theory is seen as advocating a view of texts and of the production of texts which is overly deterministic, reductive and mechanistic. Genre theory shares with liberal individualism a view of individuals as 'centred': however, the former sees individuals as socially 'produced', in structures of power, and in ideology, and therefore as socially 'centred', whereas the latter sees individuals as biologically and psychologically produced, and as psychologically centred.

In fact, this external critique of genre theory constitutes one major area of debate within genre theory itself. There the debate ranges from a position which treats genres as fully determined in all essential characteristics and therefore as outside the scope of effective individual action, to positions which treat genres as relatively fluid structures, subject to the actions of socially located individual agents. In this view the fluidity of genre derives from a complex of social factors. So, for instance, if genre is seen as the form of text which is the product of particular complex social interactions, then the degree of fluidity which inheres in social interactions lends fluidity to the form of text produced. This view does not ignore the existence of knowledge about prior texts from similar occasions, that is, knowledge of genre; rather it attempts to focus both on those factors which provide for fluidity and on those which provide for conformity and closure.

Beyond this quite fundamental debate there are other significant points of difference. These tend to focus on relatively more formal aspects: for instance, is genre the category which describes all that there is (to know) in text? That is, is a full generic description equivalent to a full description of a text in terms of (socially) meaningful and significant factors? Or is genre one particular aspect of the organization of text, one among several, each of which responds to particular and distinctly different aspects of social structures?

## Difference and closure

Narrative and argument, as cultural textual forms, provide sharply contrasting means of dealing with the same – fundamental – social and cultural issue: how to accommodate difference, contestation, conflict around salient social and cultural values in any domain, and provide integrative rather than fissive resolutions of such differences. Narrative and argument are, from this point of view, likely to be forms common to all cultures. My interest is to uncover how these textual forms appear, and are used, in one particular society. For instance, so-called literate societies will have a different set of textual forms available than so-called oral cultures. (I use 'so-called' to draw attention to the fact that many groups in literate societies are in effect 'oral' cultures.)

Within any one cultural group there is likely to be a range of differing forms of narrative and of argument, depending on the demands of specific social occasions and social structures, and, more particularly, on the prominence and persistence over time, the stability, of those occasions and structures. So, for instance, narrative might appear in an oral culture in the generic form of 'story', or of 'anecdote', or of 'epic'. Argument might appear in the textual form of 'debate', or of 'discussion', or of 'quarrel'. The availability of the everyday labels is itself an indication of a widespread and common-sense recognition, and therefore of the ubiquity and the stability of these forms.

Each of these forms is a particular response to specific, and specifically different, social occasions and social structures. An 'anecdote' presupposes a particular set of relations of speaker and hearers, with a specific level of formality, which is itself related to the institutional place where the form occurs. A 'debate' assumes a quite different set of relations among the participants to those of a 'quarrel'; and their institutional place differs. A committee may be a perfectly usual place for a 'debate' or a 'discussion'; it would produce great awkwardness if it became the location for a 'quarrel' – which is not to say that this cannot or does not happen, but rather to say that the perceived awkwardness is an indication that the expected set of social relationships has been altered.

In this chapter I will deal with argument and narrative in one cultural domain: in the institution of education, and in its concern with literacy. In particular, I will attempt to describe some of the ways in which language enters, via the production of texts, into the constitution of knowledge generally and in the school disciplines in particular. This involves some discussion of the category of *text*, specifically as to what it is that needs to be known by teachers and by students about text. I sketch in some factors beyond 'genre' which I consider essential components of a full and adequate understanding of texts, including discussion of the nature of narrative and of argument as textual forms.

All cultures need the categories of narrative and argument for dealing with two opposing, contradictory demands. On the one hand, a culture needs to provide institutionalized means of handling difference. Without difference there can be neither change nor new systems of values. Argument provides, in culture-specific textual forms, the means for bringing difference into existence. At the same time, it provides conventionalized textual forms not just for maintaining and tolerating difference, but for culturally productive use of difference. Yet where there is only difference, the cultural group cannot attain stability, cannot reproduce itself or its values. Narrative, as a textual form, provides means of resolution of difference, of reproducing, in an uncontentious mode, the forms and meanings of a culture. Narrative serves as a major means of the reproduction of social and cultural forms and values.

Narrative, in other words, is a form whose fundamental characteristic is to produce closure; argument is the form whose fundamental characteristic is to produce difference and hence openness. From this point of view narrative – or better, the many kinds of generic form in which narrative appears – is a conservative cultural form; and argument – the many kinds of generic form in which argument appears – is a progressive cultural form. Both are essential social and cultural forms: the one as the form which is productive of stability, concerned essentially with the effective reproduction of culture; the other as the form which is productive of change, concerned essentially with the effective production of new cultural values and knowledge.

Clearly, questions around knowledge or systems of value can be presented via either narrative or argumentative generic forms: that is, there is a choice to be made. The effect of using the one rather than the other will be to provide resolution and closure rather than difference and critique. Such a choice will be of quite fundamental importance in any social group. It may indeed serve as an indicator, a diagnostic device indicating differing orientations of social and cultural groups.

In the institution of education this distinction is absolutely crucial: the difference between the reproduction of salient areas of culture, on the one hand, and the production of new knowledge or new sets of values, on the other (or at the least the possibility of the production of change), is at the very basis of debate on the role of the education system in any one society.

## Narrative, argument and education

In my own work I use the notion of genre to describe those aspects of text which are the result of structurings of the immediate social context and of the occasion in which the text is produced. To take a simple example: an interview is a social occasion with particular participants (interviewers, interviewee), in a particular institution, say a firm wishing to employ a new manager. The social structure, the set of social relations, the purposes of the participants as well as their knowledge of interviews as social occasions and the kinds of language characteristic of the occasion, all of these will lead to the production of a text, namely the language used in that occasion. The text will show, in its linguistic forms, the structures, purposes, social relations (differences in power, for example) which characterize that occasion. These are the characteristics of text which I regard as generic, as giving rise to the genre 'interview'. Notice that in this description it is immaterial what the interview was about; for instance, it does not matter whether the firm was a firm of builders, or a supermarket. That is, content, so to speak, forms no part of the definition of a genre.

To take a different example: an essay in later years in high school, or at university, is a text produced in a particular social institution, on a particular occasion, which presupposes a complex set of participants – the student-writer, the teacher-reader, the discipline in which the essay occurs, the demands of that discipline, the institution of education, etc. – all with their differing purposes. The genre of essay is a text which responds to these various demands. Content is, again, relatively separate or even irrelevant from the point of view of the generic structure of this text. The student-writer's competence (within the discipline) is assessed as much by her or his competence in controlling and reproducing the appropriate generic form as it is by control of content – to the extent that that can be a separate matter.

Genre is that category which describes that aspect of textual structuring which is due to the structuring of social relations among the participants in the social occasion within which the text is being produced. Given that narrative and argument occur in distinctively different forms, depending on the 'structuring of social relations among the participants in the social occasion', that is, given that they occur in different generic form, it follows that narrative and argument are *not* generic categories. Rather, they provide a distinctively different mode of (textual) organization, one which derives from broader cultural structures. Hence it is possible to speak of narrative and argumentative genres, that is, to describe the intersection of the separate structurings of genre and of narrative and argument. In other words, narrative and argument are distinctive and independently variable modes of the structuring of text.

Narrative and argument are cultural textual categories which code fundamentally different ways of organizing salient or problematic cultural materials. Argument – in particular generic forms – is that mode of textual organization which, in a ritualized fashion, sharpens difference, and provides means for the production of texts constituted in difference. At the same time, it provides conventionalized forms of resolution of difference. These may be extra-textual, as when a parliamentary debate is brought to (temporary) resolution by a vote. In argumentative genres resolution, closure, is generally brought about extra-textually; that is, by the intervention of some authority or event external to the text. For instance, when the host of a television debate declares, 'Well, that has been most stimulating; unfortunately we've run out of time', closure is imposed, externally, temporarily. Narrative – again in particular generic forms – is that mode of textual organization which flattens and resolves difference, in a ritualized (textual) fashion. It provides means for the production of texts which are constituted around the resolution of difference, and the provision of closure. The resolution in this case comes from within the text, so that resolution is neither overtly visible nor problematic.

Narrative is not the only form of textual organization which works towards resolution of difference, towards closure. In fact most written genres tend to work in this manner, with differences which are nevertheless significant. Expository texts – essays, for instance – are constructed around difference. Typically an essay topic demands that the writer should describe and reconcile competing accounts of a particular problem. Other textual types suppress the appearance of difference quite vigorously: reports, for instance, do not set up structures of difference, but demand univocal descriptions and/or classifications of sets of phenomena.

Generally speaking, argumentative genres are more common in speech – debate, discussion, argument, quarrel – than in writing. This means that within education, based as it is on the privileged position of writing, argumentative genres are less common, less valued, than genres which tend towards resolution and closure. Nevertheless it remains an important question to ask to what extent the various written genres in schools do foreground closure or difference. Closely associated with this is the question about the extent to which different disciplines or subject areas emphasize the one rather than the other kind of text.

To take the three examples so far mentioned: a narrative type of genre such as the usual form of a scientific journal article, an essay, and a report: each of these will treat difference in a distinctive manner. The scientific paper proceeds in the characteristic form of the narrative: it describes a particular theoretical domain, identifies a problem, suggests or reports an experiment which deals with the problem, and describes the resultant effect on the broader theory. Here a problem is resolved by being reassimilated into a pre-existing single paradigm, which may itself be somewhat changed as a result. In the essay, on the other hand, contending theoretical positions may be put forward. The writer, as theoretician, has to construct a position for herself or himself (and for the reader, by implication) *vis-à-vis* these positions, and by careful assessment of available evidence reach a resolution of the problem, no matter how temporary this might be. Lastly, the report, while it may describe intractable phenomena, does not focus on these as constituting difference as such, and resolution is achieved by the device of assigning the phenomena described to pre-existing theoretical categories, in conformity with a pre-existing generic schema.

Certain disciplines construct themselves and their domain in terms of a relatively unproblematic relation both to reality and to theory, and consequently are orientated more towards textual forms of closure. One defence of the subject/discipline of English that can be made in this context is that it is that subject in the high-school curriculum which has the strongest orientation towards the most 'open' of these textual forms, namely the essay. It may be that in terms of spoken genres it is English, too, which places most emphasis on argumentative types of text. This distinction among subjects/disciplines may also be translatable into a temporal scale, so that the emphasis on argumentative types of text is least marked in the early years of schooling (coincidentally also the period of the predominance of 'the story' as the major generic type), and is most evident – even in those disciplines which make least use of them – in the later years of schooling, or at university.

Clearly, what is at issue here are modes or forms of knowledge, and fundamental assumptions about the nature of knowledge and about possibilities of producing knowledge. This is one reason why I do not subscribe to one possible reading of the conjunction of the terms 'narrative' and 'argument', namely a reading which would treat narrative as vehicle ('how I say what I want to say') and argument as content ('what I want to say'). Such a reading would seem, to me, to misrepresent in the most fundamental manner the entirely intermeshed character of means of representation and of that which is represented: in short, to misrepresent the way in which language as text is involved in the production of knowledge.

## What else is there?: a brief descriptive analysis of two high-school essays

Narrative, as I have attempted to show, is just one of a range of types of text through which knowledge can be constructed and presented. Here I wish to analyse briefly one other non-narrative type of text – an expository type, the essay – to draw out what factors beyond categories such as exposition (the cultural text type) or essay (the generic label) need to be attended to in any serious discussion of text. I will look very briefly at two factors not so far discussed: the effects of the difference between speech and writing on the presentation of knowledge; and the systematic organization of knowledge from within a particular institution, that of social science.

The two texts considered come from Year 12 (the matriculation year) of the New South Wales high-school system; they were written as part of trials for the Higher School Certificate (HSC), the final school-leaving examination. The essay entitled 'Need for tax reform in Australia' was written by a male student, whom I shall call Bob, and the essay entitled 'Need for taxation reform' by a female student, whom I shall call Jenny.

*Question 22: need for tax reform in Australia*
The main pattern of the Australian tax system is a heavy reliance on income tax, it has a tendency to cause inflation. It also has relied on partly the keynisian policies, the equity of the system has left something to be desired causing uneven income distribution and other problems. Recent suggestions for improving the system, which were outlined in the Sydney Morning Herald in 'Tax and You' are a capital gains tax, Broad Based Indirect tax system, Retail tax, wealth tax and Gift and Death duties. All of the above taxes have major problems in trying to implement them.

The heavy reliance on personal income tax is because of the decreasing reliance on other taxes and it is a big revenue collector. From 1948 to 1983/84 it has increased approximately 9.2%, i.e. from 42%–51.2%. A decrease in company tax from 15.4% in 1948 to 10% in 1983/84 is because the government has tried to get the companies to increase production, eventually leading to an expanding economy.

The reason why this system causes inflation is because they tried to adopt old methods for different and new problems, i.e. keynisian policies which were to get the government to increase revenue to companies in form of investment which needs increased production leads to increase in living standard which leads to savings. This didn't work because we have high unemployment and high prices, 'STAGFLATION'.

The equity is uneven income distribution, hitting the low income earner worse, because they spend a bigger proportion of their income than the high income earner who spend it on luxury goods. With the uneven incomes the lower strikes for pay, increasing production costs, which have to be passed on as higher prices which tend to lead to business going elsewhere.

The recent suggestion to improve the system where new taxes aimed at hitting the big income earner most of these new taxes also implement a tax evasion plan, i.e. to decrease it. The new taxes also implement a tax evasion plan, i.e. to decrease it. The new taxes involve in bringing about the evening out of incomes. The Broad Based indirect tax (BBIT) aims at the luxury goods, the capital gain aims at big investment, Retail tax at the luxury goods, the capital gain aims at big investment, Retail tax at the companies? Gift and death duties at aged and the wealth tax at everybody, so these new implementations which are supposed to be fair hit everybody.

*Question 22: need for taxation reform*
The recent call for taxation reform in Australia has been prompted by the fact that

Australia's taxation system is becoming less equitable. Therefore, the major consideration for tax reform in Australia is the equity of the new system.

At present Australia's tax system relies fairly heavily on the tax receipts from PAYE taxpayers. Their share of the total taxation revenue has increased from 42% in 1948/49 to 51.2% in 1983/84. This has been combined with a fall in taxation revenue from Company tax and custom duty. This heavy burden bourne by personal income taxpayers in Australia has been one of the major reasons for the call for tax reform. So, at present, we have a tax system that relies heavily on income tax.

The equity of Australia's tax system has also been questioned. Twenty years ago you had to earn 17.6 times the average weekly earnings (AWE) before you fell into the then top tax bracket of 66c in the dollar. Today this figure has fallen to approximately 2 times the AWE. This has meant that people in the middle income groups have fallen into the top tax bracket. So, in the past a pay rise for all Australian workers left the poor generally better off, didn't affect the rich much, but the middle income groups 'got it in the neck'. Their incomes (by no means gigantic) pushed them into the top tax bracket.

This factor was also combined with the fact that the proportion of the total income tax revenue paid by the 'rich' (with earnings more than 4 times AWE) has fallen from 48.1% in 1953/54 to a tiny 16% in 1983/84. As mentioned above this decrease was paid for by the middle income groups. This inequity of the tax system was another reason for reform.

It is very easy to criticize our tax system, but the real question is 'What can we do to make it better?' There have been several suggestions put forward, the major ones being the introduction of a retail tax, capital gains tax, gift and death duties in combination with a reformed income tax system.

A retail tax works in the following way. It is a tax which is placed on all goods and services produced in a community. It is levied at a flat rate. Because it is levied at a flat rate, it is regressive in nature.

Capital gains tax is a tax paid on the capital gain, i.e. the difference between the price at which you sell an item and the price at which you bought it.

Bob's text 'Need for tax reform' (the incorrect title) is more speech-like, more colloquial than Jenny's (correct) 'Need for taxation reform'. So, for instance, the first sentence of Bob's essay has a characteristically speech-like structure of *main clause adjoined to main clause*: '. . . reliance on income tax, it has a tendency . . .'. In spoken language the link between the two clauses would be carried intonationally. When a structure such as this appears in writing, however, it is perceived as 'not properly connected', and above all, as 'not a proper sentence'. Given that the sentence is the quintessentially characteristic unit of written language, the absence of 'proper sentences' therefore leaves a sense of inappropriateness, insufficiency. Such judgements are unlikely to be analysed or articulated by the reader (teacher); it is most likely that they will emerge as judgements not about language, but about the intellectual capabilities of the writer, and his abilities as an economist. The second sentence is another instance of this speech-like structure; there are other instances throughout the text, even though they are by no means the major form. A different instance of speech-like grammar is the use here of the '. . . is because . . .' form: 'The heavy reliance . . . is because of the decreasing . . .'. The 'is because' form is common in spoken English – 'It's because you never listen . . .'. In writing, however, this kind of causal connection tends to be made by the use of the verb 'cause': 'the decreasing reliance . . . caused the heavy . . .'. There is a very clear difference between Bob and Jenny's texts from this point of view: Jenny's essay has very few of the more speech-like forms.

The point to be made here is that a mode of written presentation which draws on grammatical forms which are more appropriate in spoken genres leads, or can lead, to a negative valuation of the content, a particular assessment of the writer's knowledge of the subject matter, and of his standing in the discipline. Judgements on language, made quite intuitively, can become judgements about the users of language. This is a matter of genre, as it involves the use of language more appropriate to spoken genres in a genre belonging to the set of written genres. But perhaps this matter is best seen as another distinct and independently variable factor, the broad and fundamental distinction of speech and writing.

My next point, the systematic *linguistic* organization of knowledge within particular disciplines, is also a separate question to genre in my theory of text. This is the domain which I label 'discourse', following the work of Foucault. Here I will focus on two aspects of this discourse: the manner in which typical relations and practices in this domain are represented, and the manner in which the scientist/investigator's position has to be constructed linguistically.

In the two essays the most frequent type of clause is one which establishes a relation between two entities: X is Y. For instance, from Bob's essay, 'The main pattern . . . is a heavy reliance', or, from Jenny's essay 'the major consideration . . . is the equity of . . .'. This type of clause relates one category to another, classifies and explains by classifying: 'You want to know what the main pattern is? It is a heavy reliance on . . .'. The relational clause is one part of a cultural/textual system for assimilating areas which are unknown and therefore problematic for a discipline, to those areas which are, from the discipline's view, established and secure. The ability to operate this system competently and appropriately marks the writer either as a member of or as an aspirant to the community defined by the discipline.

Both writers use this system competently, one exception being the first sentence in Bob's essay: 'a heavy reliance' is not a 'pattern'. In cases such as this where a relation of (near) equivalence has to be established between items which are not equivalent, the mechanisms available in writing are the *is-substitutes*. Here, for instance, *shows* would have served that function: 'the pattern . . . shows a heavy reliance . . .'. Generally speaking, the ability to use is-substitutes is a requirement of writing in disciplines of this kind. There are many alternatives: *have* ('these taxes have major problems' = 'there are major problems with'); *outline* ('. . . were outlined in the *Sydney Morning Herald*' = 'which appeared/were in the *SMH*'); *increase, bear,* etc. The ability to use these forms establishes the writer *both* as an 'accomplished writer' and as an effective practitioner of the discipline, one who understands subtle distinctions and nuances, and knows how to control them. The range of forms, moreover, makes the disciplinary practices seem diverse: not simply 'X is Y', but 'X has Y', 'X shows Y', 'X displays Y', etc. Verbs such as *show*, *display* also have a transitive force, and with that the appearance of 'real' activity rather than mere classification.

On this last dimension, the use of is-substitutes, there is a clear difference between the two essays: Jenny's essay shows greater diversity and control than Bob's.

It should be clear that these factors have an effect in relation to the production of knowledge, and in relation to the position of the scientist/writer. The writer who has more forms at her or his disposal appears not only as the more accomplished writer, but also as the economist/scientist who is able to make more, and more discriminating, more discerning and more finely nuanced judgements. Linguistic ability here becomes disciplinary power. It may be the first step in explaining why Jenny's essay received a grade of 18 out of 20, and Bob's 12 out of 20.

These are factors which are, in my theory of text, outside the generic. Before concluding this section, I will briefly make some reference to one aspect of generic structuring, namely the writer's construction of an impersonal voice, an impersonal speaking position. Impersonality in these two texts arises in two ways: one, which is outside genre, has to do with the place of the writer and scientist within the discipline. This is a matter of discourse, in my terms, and is the point I have just attended to above. The second, which is generic, has to do with the writer's position *qua* writer, that is, in her or his relation with a specific reading audience.

An example of impersonality of the second type would be, from Bob's essay: 'The reason why this system causes inflation . . .'. Here the writer addresses the reader directly, in explaining to the reader – who is constructed by the writer as someone who needs to know – what the reason is.

The address to the reader has to do, directly, with the structures of the social occasion in which the text is being produced. It is, therefore, in my terms, clearly an aspect of generic structure. These are factors which remain constant irrespective of content. An example from Jenny's text is: 'Therefore, the major consideration for tax reform . . . is . . .'; this is similar in function to Bob's 'The reason . . . is . . .'. Another example (again from Jenny's essay) is: 'Australia's tax system relies fairly heavily on the tax receipts . . .'. 'Fairly' indicates a qualification which may be the economist's cautious qualification (and therefore a matter of discourse) or it may be the student/writer's awareness of the greater power and knowledge of the teacher/reader: protection, as it were, against the greater knowledge of the teacher. In the latter case, it is part of the social structure of the occasion of writing, and therefore a generic matter.

In general, any linguistic form which 'reveals' the writer's position or point of view has the effect of, literally, suggesting subjectivity, and a text which manages to suppress evidence of the writer's position has the effect of suggesting objectivity. The writer's task is to manage these indicators in accordance with the always specific demands of any one discipline, or, more broadly speaking, of the kind of writing being attempted. Objectivity can then appear as objectivity either about subject matter or about the writer–reader relationship, or both, leading to distinct types of impersonality.

The writer's task, as I said, is to manage the two kinds of indicator of impersonality (or indeed of 'personality') quite precisely. Good management suggests control and clarity both in the individual's relation to knowledge, and in her or his relation to the reader in mediating that knowledge. On the whole, Jenny is a better manager than Bob, who frequently blurs the two kinds of impersonality, as for instance in the 'is because' form, which conflates the 'X is Y' form of the scientist, with the role of explainer (the 'because') of the writer.

## Conclusion: writers, knowledge, and texts

Jenny and Bob are faced, in their HSC trials, with a complex task; at the very least they have to fulfil three quite distinct demands: to demonstrate familiarity or inwardness with the discipline; to convey knowledge about this discipline both to an ostensibly non-disciplinary audience ('the general reader') *and* to a disciplinary reader in the person of the teacher; and to meet the assessment requirements of the discipline, and of the educational institution, merged again in the person of the teacher. Success in the performance of all three tasks together will lead to the institution's final judgement on the writer: as an appropriate (aspirant) member of the discipline, and as someone who is aware of the complexities of social structures and power. All these tend to play their part in the assessment of the writer as a competent, knowledgeable social being.

In any text a number of factors come together, all of which play their role in how the text presents, represents, constructs its world – or better, how a writer achieves this in the writing of a text (or a speaker in the interactive construction of a spoken text). Texts are, literally, weaves of categories of different kinds. Categories like narrative, exposition, argument, deal with the basic cultural problem of how to deal with difference – either by providing textual forms that work towards closure in a variety of ways, or which work towards a culturally productive use of difference. Others – generic categories such as essay, children's story, scientific paper, debate, discussion, chat – deal with the interrelation of language and quite specific social occasions in which language plays a prominent role. Yet others, discourses such as economics, law, English, gender, nationalism, deal with the manner in which social institutions organize cultural values and knowledge in the light of their own meanings and structures. Last, and by no means least, all texts must appear in either the mode of writing or of speech – or of particular socially produced mixes of these.

In all of these, social agents as writers or as speakers take their position and play their part. All of these are affected by the practices of individuals as social agents;

all of them exert the force of their meanings on individual writers and speakers. Producing successful texts – that is, texts which serve the purposes of the speaker or writer – demands a knowledge of these factors, a critical awareness of their meaning and their potential, of the freedom and of the constraints that speakers and writers experience in their making of texts.

# 2 Argument as social action

PETER MEDWAY

> If we are told that all squares are four-sided figures we know at once that some four-sided figures are squares. (But it would be wrong to infer that all four-sided figures are squares.) . . .
>
> If we are assured that some birds are thieves we can infer that some thieves are birds. The one truth implies the other.
>
> If we are informed that all elms are trees we can infer that things which are not trees cannot possibly be elms.
>
> All these are obvious enough. We call them immediate inferences because we arrive at them immediately. Nevertheless people do frequently make false inferences. . . .
>
> Say what can be truthfully inferred from the following: . . . (c) No policeman is a trade unionist . . .
>
> Read through a leading article in any daily paper, write out a brief summary, and examine the lines of argument (Marriott 1923, pp. 41–5).

English was once quite concerned with thinking and specifically with argument. Marriott (1923, pp. 6–7), acknowledging that 'Teachers will frequently disagree with statements contained in the book', explains:

> That is part of the plot! Disagreement is as necessary for a flow of connected thought as is difference of potential for a movement of electricity. . . . When a boy begins to say what he thinks instead of trying to think what he shall say he becomes interesting in proportion as he is interested. The English teacher's greatest difficulty is the apparent absence of ideas on the part of the class. When thought begins to stir within the pupils' minds the power of expression seems to be generated spontaneously.

Claims which more recently have been made for the role of experience in English – that tapping into deeply felt experience releases powers of expression – were thus in those days made for the role of ideas and beliefs activated by argument. But Marriott is not simply concerned with pedagogical techniques for eliciting motivated language. (His book is intended not only for English lessons but more generally 'For use in day schools, evening classes, adult classes etc.')

Although '[the] Education Act of 1870 taught the whole nation to read, and to-day the illiterate person is an anachronism', the task is unfinished: 'The nation has been taught to absorb: it has not learnt to analyse or construct' (Marriott 1923, pp. 5–6). Thus while the bulk of the chapters are about true and false thinking and argument (e.g. 'How some people argue', 'Deductive reasoning', 'Rival hypotheses', 'Concerning evidence', 'Cause and effect'), the final chapters deal with 'The springs of action' ('it is a huge mistake to suppose that we are "reasonable" beings' (p. 150)), 'Man as a social animal' ('It is the duty of every intelligent citizen to think about the government of the country and to improve it whenever and wherever he can' (p. 155)), 'Democracy' (which requires 'men who will be independent and refuse to listen to "war-cries" . . . Think for yourself!' (p. 158)) and 'Utopia' ('The person who is not interested in these great dreams is little better than a tailor's dummy' (p. 162)).

The historians of English teaching in England and Wales, while noting the importance of both grammar and literature, have overlooked the centrality of *rationality* as a guiding concept in particularly the grammar school version of the subject. In the grammar school I attended, 'precision of thought' (or 'clear thinking') was a prime value, while a point of particular praise was having 'a lively mind' – neither of them phrases one associates with post-Leavisite 'personal growth' teachers in the comprehensive schools of the 1960s and 1970s. The grammar school ethos was well summed up by Frances Stevens (1960, p. 104), who noted

> an emphasis on clear and independent thinking, which is also associated by some with the development of precise expression in speech and writing. The acquisition of powers of criticism and judgement is felt to be important. The practice of intellectual discipline is widely praised.

Marriott's book was in sufficient demand to be reprinted in 1924 but I do not know how widespread was the sort of teaching of logic which it supported. By the 1950s, one form in which the value of rationality was promoted was the 'argumentative essay'. Typical topics were caricatured by Harold Rosen (1958, p. 92), a grammar school teacher who had recently moved to a comprehensive: 'What about the problems created by TV, admass, subtopia, the colour bar, competitive international sport? What about Culture, Economics, Society, Life, Time and the Cosmos?' The new movement which gathered pace in English in the 1960s, concentrating on the concrete particulars of immediate and remembered experience and practising a Lawrentian avoidance of generalities, meant that the generalizing essay and thinking in general, in the sense of an intellectual activity operating on ideas and derived knowledge, fell from favour. The end of GCE may have been the blow which finally killed off the practice.

The generalizing O-level essay certainly had little going for it, and the token piece of 'discursive writing' on capital or corporal punishment, smoking, school uniform or fox-hunting, is one of the least loved elements of contemporary English. Nevertheless, in the abandonment of a more general concern with rationality and quality of thinking and argument, it is hard not to feel that something important has been lost. So much argument goes on around us, in the media, in everyday life and in workplaces, that there seems every point in helping pupils assess it critically. Moreover, Marriott's book, which attempted to do just that, was fun as well as being useful (if sexist), suggesting that approaches rather livelier than the argumentative essay are possible. And without begging any questions about the sort of democracy we live in, it is undeniable that argument is at the heart of the democratic process and that lack of reason and logic may be socially harmful. Moreover, placing rationality at the heart of the subject when that was, at least in the rhetoric, the guiding value of liberal education, meant that English was visibly central to the curriculum, whereas it has since marginalized itself in an idiosyncratic enclave of concern for the personal and affective.

Perhaps the main reason why the tradition prizing rationality disappeared was the abolition of the grammar schools, mainly in the 1960s and 1970s. A regime based on detached analysis and intellectual effort was judged unsuitable for the majority of pupils in the new comprehensive schools. But there were other, well-founded objections to it. The strength of the new approach to English was that its activities were based on 'naturally' occurring processes. It took the recounting, the reminiscing and the re-enacting which children constantly engaged in, at least internally, and the everyday language they used in sharing their experiences, and intensified them, making them (especially by leading them into writing) more powerful, more subtle and more discriminating. Institutionalized school argument, on the other hand, in the form of essays and debates, was an artificial growth without roots in everyday discourse. Its topics were typically general and remote and unrelated to pupils' preoccupations.

Thus, even if the importance of argument were acknowledged, the practices purporting to develop it were unacceptable. The problem lay with the pedagogy, not with the nature of argument. Argument arises as naturally in the world's discourse as does narrative; indeed, it often arises out of and is embedded within narrative. Accounts, including narrative accounts, have in any case more in common with argument than is generally supposed. Providing the accounts occur in real discourse (other than fiction) and are actually said or written by someone to someone, whether a face-to-face interlocutor or a general readership, in speech-act terms they are assertions, made within the conventional understanding that what is stated is not arbitrary but can be justified and that questioning or rebuttal as well as acceptance are legitimate responses. Thus even narratives and descriptions of states of affairs, events and situations are in a sense arguments, asserting challengeable claims about the truth of what is represented, the significance ascribed to it and the rightness of the values which underlie the selection of the topic for recounting and its interpretation.

Accounts in fiction, of course, and indeed many stories told in everyday exchanges, are not overtly assertions. According to Pratt (1977) they subsist in a sort of 'time out', when conversational turns are suspended, allowing the speaker (and, she claims, by extension the writer) the floor to make a longer contribution than is normally acceptable. In return for the privilege, the unspoken contract is that the narrator has to provide something of more than ordinary significance, interest or shapeliness. What the narrator typically produces is a 'display text' which *presents* some reality for contemplating, rather than a set of propositional assertions. Although the convention is, in the recounting of anecdotes at least in mainstream English and American culture, that one ends with a statement indicating the point of the story, everyone understands that the point is not really in this final propositionally presented moral or teaching but in the story as a whole. Novels, of course, may dispense with the concluding message altogether.

Nevertheless, it is now increasingly held that even novels function as assertions or argumentative claims. Although what is asserted is implicit in the whole rather than stated in any particular passage, some critics are quite clear that the view of literature as without referent and as constituting a detached world of its own is wrong. In the first place, it simply fails to account for, or consigns to subliterary status, a mass of texts such as *Uncle Tom's Cabin* which were written precisely to show people what the world was like and to mobilize opinion for a particular course of action.

> In modernist thinking, literature is by definition a form of discourse that has no designs on the world. It does not attempt to change things, but merely to represent them, and it does so in a specifically literary language whose claim to value lies in its uniqueness. Consequently, works whose stated purpose is to influence the course of history, and which therefore employ a language that is not only not unique but common and accessible to everyone, do not qualify as works of art (Tompkins 1981, p. 82; quoted by Reising 1986, p. 247).

In the second place, even classic American novels which have traditionally been judged to be peculiarly unanchored in American social reality (*Moby Dick*, for instance) are now claimed by Reising to be very much about the 'social processes and relationships' of the society, and in particular the recent fact of slavery.

Verbal representations of all kinds, then, assume the legitimacy of and may be the occasion for comeback of various types, including supplementary or alternative accounts, the explication of implications, the expression of sympathy or concurrence – or argument: disputation, challenge and counter-assertion. Narratives, we now see, often embody arguments, and sometimes they are offered in support of an argument, the argument coming first and then the narrative. Accounts offered in everyday discourse, as opposed to literary writing, are typically mixed in both function and form. Evaluative comments, perceived implications, judgemental asides of tenuous relevance, insults and longings may all be expressed in the course of telling someone how it is or how it was. Speculation may also be included: reflective wondering, provisional sense-making, tentative hypothesis-suggesting and curious question-raising. Put another way, everyday oral accounts present not a smooth face of settled fact but a bumpy surface allowing plenty for the interlocutor later to seize hold of as the basis for reciprocal comment or challenge.

In contrast with the argumentative essay, then, it would be good to see argument arising in that sort of way, as part of the normal business of giving accounts and responding to them. In English lessons in the United Kingdom, however, written narratives do not appear to be like that. At least in a sample I examined closely, personal writing offers *only* representation without comments, questions, hypotheses or overt claims (Medway 1986). It follows a literary model in which the Leavisite criterion – that the particulars, if adequately presented, should speak for themselves – operates. In the last thirty years we seem simply to have switched, from generalizing essays which are all ideas and no represented reality to personal writing which is all experienced particulars and no ideas, as if you can only choose between narrative and argument and cannot engage in both at once.

What is needed, then, is to bring thinking back into personal writing, so that it presents not only re-enactments of experience but also related thoughts which might constitute initial moves in arguments – or in inquiries or speculations or explorations. Writers need to posit ideas as well as represent things. Conversely, as well as writing about experience being set up in such a way as to initiate argument, argument needs to be about issues that matter to writers and relate to their experience, however broadly defined. The best context will be one in which participants share a common social experience. Hardcastle (1985, p. 21) cites a pupil's poem

> which can be shown to have its origins in the arguments which the class conducted with itself over a number of years. What began as a forceful [spoken] statement intended to settle an argument about the place of Caribbean history in the syllabus, made with the warrant of personal history behind it, was subsequently internalised and underwent an inward change before making its appearance several months later as a rather scrappy first draft.

A couple of other comments by Hardcastle (1985, p. 19) are worth noting:

> By this stage the class, now in its fourth year, had three years' experience of regular discussion work behind it. The intentions and the inferences they made as listeners depended on their sharing tacit frames of reference carried forward from their interactions.

This was a class, in other words, which had lived together; they were a group with much more between them than the accident of being placed together for one curriculum subject out of many in the week. Their arguments, like the one about the teaching of Caribbean history which gave rise, much later, to the poem, were sometimes continued in writing. Given a choice of what to write, some pupils sometimes chose to write down, in 'position papers', the points they were making, or wished they had made, or now on reflection wanted to make, in the oral discussion.

This example allows us to bring a new dimension into our own argument. In

Hardcastle's classroom argument was not a contained and timetabled activity, a regular assignment like the weekly essay, but flowed through the life of the class, just as outside school argument is typically part of life's business, and not just something for moments of withdrawal. In such argument much may be at stake in the attempt to convince or persuade, so that what matters is not presenting the better case but getting the other person to change: anything less is failure. Hardcastle's pupils argued the way they sometimes did because they desperately wanted one or more of their peers to *see* something which they themselves could see. What counted was less logic than rhetoric, less the merits of the presented case than the achievement of effects in the audience. It mattered to change the views in question because the views were, potentially at any rate, linked to action. As Benjamin Franklin (1964, pp. 64–5) eventually concluded, an argumentative technique that logically confounds the opposition may not in the real world be what brings the greatest advantage to the person seeking to affect the *actions* of others:

> While I was intent on improving my Language, I met with an English Grammar (I think it was Greenwood's) at the End of which there were two little Sketches on the Arts of Rhetoric and Logic, the latter finishing with a Specimen of a Dispute in the Socratic Method. And soon after I procur'd Xenophon's *Memorable Things of Socrates*, wherein there are many Instances of the same Method. I was charm'd with it, adopted it, dropt my abrupt Contradiction, and positive Argumentation, and put on the humble Enquirer and Doubter. And being then, from reading Shaftesbury and Collins, made a real Doubter in many Points of our Religious Doctrine, I found this Method safest for my self and very embarassing to those against whom I used it, therefore I took a Delight in it, practis'd it continually, and grew very artful and expert in drawing People even of superior Knowledge into Concessions the Consequences of which they did not foresee, entangling them in Difficulties out of which they could not extricate themselves, and so obtaining Victories that neither myself nor my Cause always deserved.
>
> I continu'd this Method some few Years, but gradually left it, retaining only the Habit of expressing my self in Terms of modest Diffidence, never using when I advance any thing that may possibly be disputed, the Words, *Certainly*, *undoubtedly*, or any others that gave the Air of Positiveness to an Opinion; but rather say, I conceive, or I apprehend a Thing to be so or so, It appears to me, or I should think it so or so for such and such Reasons, or I imagine it to be so, or it is so if I am not mistaken. This Habit I believe has been of great Advantage to me.

Two areas of theory can help at this point to make some distinctions clearer. Hardcastle (1965, p. 18) himself invokes discourse theory: 'We must see that the poem occupies a space in the discourses of the classroom which have been built over time, and in relation to the wider discourses about Caribbean history.' Language which actually happens, which gets transacted, as opposed to language which exists merely as inert linguistic form (such as sentences for parsing) is a transaction between people in specific circumstances with specific purposes and in relation to specific practices. The term 'discourse' acknowledges that language is embedded in social action as one means by which action is realized. Hardcastle's pupils were not merely 'mounting arguments'; they were getting each other to change their minds, so that they could gain support from others for their own beliefs, take common attitudes towards matters which were important to them and maybe change the world in a small way.

Even literature can be brought within this concept of discourse, according to some recent critics and theorists. There is never no social context for writing, and more texts than we have traditionally recognized were written as contributions not to 'literature' but to some immediate worldly enterprise. According to Edward Said (1984, pp. 56–7),

> With a few exceptions, most of [Swift's] writing was precisely occasional: it was stimulated by a specific occasion and planned in some way to change it. . . . *The Conduct of the Allies* and *The Public Spirit of the Whigs* take place, as it were, in their actual dispersion on the streets of London.

Swift's political and religious tracts were 'embedded as events in a complex of events in the world' (Said 1984, p. 58). And, as I mentioned earlier, recent studies have seen in classic American literature, despite its detached appearance, a form of intervention in the society.

According to the speech-act theory developed by Austin (1962) and by Searle (1969, 1979), normal language operates at three levels. At the *locutionary* level it generates a sequence of words which constitute grammatically well-formed sentences. A text produced by, say, a sentence-combining exercise would fulfil the criteria of the locutionary level: what is produced is recognizably language and not gibberish. Such texts, however, are not speech acts: nobody is saying them and meaning them. They lack force at the *illocutionary* level. In order to count as language in the full sense, written and spoken texts need to be the realization of speech acts such as asserting, promising, claiming, denying, pardoning or joking. To oversimplify crudely, the achievement of English teaching in recent years has been to bring pupils' writing from the locutionary to the illocutionary level. The writing we seek is no longer little more than a well-formed construction deploying appropriate ideas and sentiments in approved conventional form (it has never been only that, of course). We now expect that pupils will say something they find worth saying. Mastery of Marriott's (1923) exercises will not in itself produce pupils who argue from conviction. When Stephen Clarke and John Sinker imply in this volume that in travel writing it is the 'sincerity, conviction and power' of the arguments that accounts for the pupils' engagement with them, they are referring to illocutionary features, not to logic, consistency and so on which are the locutionary aspects Marriott is concerned to impart.

The speech-act theorists specify a third level, the *perlocutionary*. This refers to the fact that language has effects on other people. If investing language with illocutionary force means meaning it, at the perlocutionary level we use our utterances as social acts to influence others, to soothe, threaten, impel, amuse, or to make people do things or stop them doing things. Thus a text which at the illocutionary level may be an expression of a feeling ('I'm not happy about your going there') may at the perlocutionary level, depending on the circumstances, be a prohibition (equivalent to 'You are not to go').

Capability in language means being able to handle language at all three levels. In English we have learnt to help pupils with the first two. On leaving us, however, our pupils, competent though they may be in articulating what they want to say, have learnt little about what to say when to whom and how, about how to deploy their language in social contexts.

We are so familiar with the way things are done in schools that we accept the familiar divisions of school writing as if they represent the entire universe of written texts. We variously classify the ground to be covered as narrative, description, exposition and argument, as transactional, expressive and poetic, as prose and poetry, as personal and impersonal, or as a host of rough-and-ready common-sense types such as story, essay, poem, play, discursive writing, description, dialogue or letter. But beyond these distinctions we are generally blind to a larger one: between writing which is disengaged from the world of actions and writing which is intended to have consequences in that world. The London Writing Research Group in the 1960s devised a theory which recognized this distinction: behind the transactional and poetic functions of writing they identified two different relationships to events: that of participant and that of spectator. Transactional writing as they defined it was writing which got things done and which advanced the world's affairs. In practice, however, they classified as transactional a vast body of school writing such as history essays, geography notes and science lab reports which got nothing done. This was unfortunate because, in the first place, such writing only *simulated* the function it purported to serve, that of informing, since no one would read it who wanted or needed the information and ideas; and, in the second place, because informing is not necessarily intended to have consequences for action.

In English, writing designed to have action consequences does appear, but invariably in simulated form. It takes two forms. One is dummy-run practice in what teachers term 'functional', 'objective', 'factual' or 'conventional' writing such as insurance claims, accident reports and factual descriptions. All but two of twenty-one second-year secondary English classes whose work over a year I examined had been set at least one piece of writing of this type, but the total number of such pieces amounted to only 20 per cent, as against 80 per cent of 'imaginative' pieces. Teachers feel obliged to make a gesture towards this work but find it boring. I saw one teacher set out with the worthiest of intentions, explaining to his first-year class that he wanted an accurate, strictly businesslike description of a room, such as a surveyor might write. As the lesson proceeded, however, and Bill and the class started enjoying themselves, the character of the room, imaginary from the start, took on zany and magical qualities. The teacher did a skit with one pupil about a tiny room in which the owner was proposing to place numerous items of very large furniture which collectively were far bigger than the room, and the writing task, when eventually specified, turned out to be 'A Strange Room'; the surveyor mode had quietly been dropped, to the evident relief of all concerned.

The other sort, pseudo-documents or simulations of ships' logs, letters from prison, school reports, newspaper items, suicide notes, police notebooks and wanted posters, usually occurs in writing based on literature as vehicles on which pupils can conduct their own imaginative explorations of the world of the story. Often these are writings which in the real world would have very definite consequences. But because their texts are not deployed in the world in the ways that the real thing would be, pupils do not have the chance to learn about the way language works as one channel of social action. They never learn whether their school report gets the parents to take action or whether the police officer's notes stand up as evidence in court.

Writing, at least in English lessons, tends to be an end in itself. Since it is agreed to be a requirement of English that writing be practised, this need is often the initiating occasion for writing to take place, although teachers who know what they are doing are aware of the necessity to find an immediate purpose which will give the activity point for the pupils. These immediate, found or devised purposes, however, are seldom about producing effects in the world of events. In good classrooms writing will certainly have audiences who will be affected, but the effect on them will be that they recognize or dispute the truth of the representation, or are reminded of aspects of their own experience, or are intrigued and captivated by the narrative or the language, or simply enjoy the reading. Again in the livelier English class, other pupils may respond verbally to a piece of writing by one of their peers, either orally or in writing, commenting, evaluating, agreeing or disagreeing, or contributing other experiences and alternative perspectives. But they will not normally as a result of receiving the written message do anything which produces changes in the configuration of the non-verbal world. They will not cancel an order, order an arrest, make a recipe, move supplies from one place to another, meet someone from a train or engage in civil disobedience.

Language in school, it seems, has always, since antiquity, been divorced from action. Rhetoric developed as an art in Greece to meet the needs of the democracy in the assembly, the law court and the ceremonial occasion such as funerals and victory speeches. By the time it became institutionalized, in Rome, as one of the three main paths of the educational *trivium*, the main political, action-related function of rhetoric had fallen into disuse with the ending of democracy. Rhetoric was from then on taught not as influencing an audience to action but as producing spoken and, later, written texts within conventional forms.

That is essentially where we have stayed, except in classrooms like John Hardcastle's. Pupils' writing may now at least say something of significance to the writer, but it does not do anything as an event in the world. It is extremely rare to find in schools examples of written language which go even as far as the following short texts in constituting messages intended to have consequences in the world of action. They were written by some fourth-year pupils in an agriculture class designed to fulfil the criteria of the Technical and Vocational Education Initiative (TVEI). The school TVEI co-ordinator, Mr M., had offered the group the help of some fifth-year pupils in getting the animal shed painted. The first note was written before the help, the second after.

> 5th years please could you paint all the radiators and pipes Green (undercoat) Please paint noticeboard (sand gold emulsion paint) and coat hangers as well. Can you also paint the shelves left of the door green When you have finish with the paints and brushes can you put them back in the box
>
> P.S please paint rim of notice board green.
>
> thanks
>
> PPPS make sure brushes are completley clean, and make a good job of it.

> To Mr M. We appreciate the work that the 5th years did apart from a few minor details such as not washing the brushes properly and also not finishing the radiators.
>
> We would be greatful if David ——
>                             Allan ——
> would come back and repaint the notice board yellow and the rim of notice board green (Green Gloss). If they have got time left please can they redo the radiators and pipes
>
> yours sincereley
>
> Andrew —— Tracey —— Becky —— Claire ——

If pupils spent less of their time in lessons and more in situations, like that of running a smallholding or newspaper, argument would be directly related to action. If schools built in a progression of situations from the earliest years, the demands which these placed on pupils would grow to the point where, in the fourth or fifth year of secondary school, developed procedures for co-operative decision-making would be essential; if the enterprise was both important and relatively complex, it might well be necessary for positions to be argued in writing. This is the direction in which TVEI, at its best, is pointing.

TVEI, however, tends to be uncritical. TVEI contexts foster argument linked to decision-making, certainly, but the argument tends to be about the best way to do things, about means rather than ends. It is, in other words, essentially technical; the values from which are derived the criteria for the decisions are themselves unexamined. The debate in which John Hardcastle's pupils were engaged, on the other hand, was not directly action-linked: they were not in a position to decide whether the curriculum would or would not include Caribbean history. It was, however, action-linked in a less immediate sense, in that the value positions they arrived at as a result of continuing debate over a long period would be capable of influencing a range of unpredicted future actions, beginning with their behaviour towards each other. A classroom culture which fosters that sort of debate about ends, about what ought to be done not only in the zone over which immediate control is exercised but also in the wider society, seems to be the background we need for engagements in practical enterprises in which values and principles, as well as technical competences and 'personal skills', might be actualized in practice.

# 3

# Divine dialogues: the role of argument in the narrative discourse of a five-year-old storyteller

CAROL FOX

And he tells the knight to come and catch
the witch      but the knight says   'No
'cos I'm on your side and I'm on the
witch's side'      'Oh so if you're on the
witch's side I have to be on the witch's
side 'cos I'm on your side'

The little syllogism above occurs in the middle of a very colourful story, spontaneously invented and told by five-and-a-half-year-old Josh. It is one story from approximately 200 which were told by five young children at home, tape-recorded by one of their parents, and sent to me as data for a study of the children's emergent narrative and literary competences. The children had heard many hundreds of stories told and read to them, and I found that their knowledge of narrative discourse and of the language of writing was unexpectedly complex and advanced for pre-school children who were not yet independently literate.

For example, by using Genette's (1972) categories of tense, mood, and voice to analyse some of the children's stories, it was possible to uncover the considerable complexity of the time relationships, the shifts in point of view, and the narrating functions, in the narratives of the two five-year-olds in the study. There is no doubt at all that these children were highly-skilled storytellers; even when the events narrated in their stories were fairly insignificant and sparse, they had their ways of 'tuning in' instantly to the discourses they knew so well from the authors and storytellers they had encountered in the past.

I have proposed elsewhere (Fox 1988) that these children, and probably most children, had had their experience of hearing and using language shaped from the beginning by metaphor. Children who have had rich experiences of verbal play and art from early infancy find themselves *not* surrounded by a unitary language which pre-exists them and they acquire, but are actively engaged in many processes of metaphor-making, taking up positions in many discourses (Walkerdine 1982) which come to be the symbols of the major affects of their lives – power, pleasure, fear, love, and so on. Among these discourses (the teacher and the pupil, the mother and the father, the nurse and the doctor and the patient) stories offer children very powerful representations of their inner and their social living. Children are able to refashion the story-metaphors they encounter to reflect their own meanings in ways which are extraordinarily finely adapted to their personal preoccupations, experiences and needs. I reiterate this point here because I am going to discuss the children's uses of argument in their stories, a discourse which, in spite of Moffett's (1968) well-known assertion that for children for a long time 'narrative must do for all', we as teachers are often inclined to see in a rarified and 'pure' realm of its own, floating, alongside 'formal operations' and 'abstract thought', well above the heads of most primary and many secondary school pupils. My story data led me to believe that argument is not a higher and later development of children's thinking, but begins its growth in the life-giving oxygen of narrative discourse and verbal play from the children's earliest encounters with stories – both those in books and those they hear all the time in everyday talk. I am suggesting that storytelling contexts which are pleasureable, emotional and metaphorical, lead children into discourses which are more rational than the term 'narrative' might at first imply.

Rosen (1988a, p. 20) proposes that a 'view of narrative which does not take account of its use in argument or any kind of conversation is bound to be an impoverished view', a suggestion that I would like to turn around, interchanging the words 'narrative' and 'argument', for what I propose, and hope to illustrate here, is that *argument is implicit in narrative discourse itself.* The emphasis here must be on *discourse*, the language used by storytellers to engage the attention of listeners, the communicative, reciprocal interaction of storytelling, the often elaborate and subtle means employed by storytellers to let us know why this story or that story is being told, or read, or written, or listened to at all. Narrative conceived as a discursive activity releases us from the straitjacket of considering it solely in terms of the events narrated, the plot, or what Rumelhart (1977, pp. 298–9) calls the 'gist' of the story. It is simplistic to view narrative as gist, as many psychologists of story recall have done; when stories are seen as 'problem-solving formats' (Rumelhart 1977, p. 269), or as 'an underlying configuration of propositions' (Thorndyke and Yekovitch 1980, p. 30) it is a simple matter to demonstrate, using controlled experiments and specially devised stories, that young children are not very good at retelling, or recalling, or even inventing them, and that, like argument itself, narrative competence is a later cognitive development. But, as Rosen (1984; 1985; 1986) has pointed out to us very clearly, narrative discourse is essentially dialogic, and it is in this respect that story discourses have embedded in them the roots of so many other discourse structures (those which are to do with physical, historical, geographical and mathematical representations of reality, for example), including the discourse of argument.

In my story data I notice two major forms of dialogic, discursive argumentation. There is one in which the child as narrator conducts a dialogue, either directly or as a more obscure unidentified narrator, with an imagined listener. Here the text that the child narrates propels itself forward with questions, hypotheses, explanations and propositions, which are essentially addressed to itself, and which make explicit the particular problems which the story must address. The second type of argumentation is in a more dramatic, showing-rather-than-telling mode, where characters in stories stop and discuss problems and their possible solutions together, as in the quotation which heads this article. This second kind of argument in narrative discourse is the storyteller's representation of the language of argument in life, and it draws on children's knowledge of conversation, not only the sort they participate in all the time, but also the more shaped, tidy and economical sort that gets transposed into written language in storybooks. Both types of argument are very clearly represented in the stories invented by five-year-old Josh. They can be illustrated from two of his earlier stories, narrated when he was just over five:

but as you know who lived in the forest?
well shall I tell you?
well it was a big wicked grey wolf
and (so-so) so how should they get away from
this forest 'cos if he saw them he would
surely swallow them up?

This story, which is loosely based on the Grimm tale, *Snow White and Rose Red*, is narrated in the third person and the past tense. Yet it is clear from the quotation that the story has a hidden narrator, never identified, who nevertheless presents the story problem in a dialogic form, posing three questions to the imagined listener, or, rather, to the narrative discourse itself, for it is the text that must answer these questions, not the listener. The first two questions are of the suspense-building kind, leading the text on towards the revelation of the 'big wicked grey wolf', whose presence is the central problem which the story must solve. This central problem is presented as a further rhetorical question, this time with a hypothesis appended to it which leaves us in no doubt about the threat the wolf represents to the family of rabbits. The hypothesis not only establishes the danger the rabbits are in, but also serves as an explanation for raising the question 'so how should they get away from this forest?'. Questions, problems, hypotheses and explanations are the tools of argumentative discourse, but here they are put to service in the narrative discourse; they are part of the structure of the story.

The second passage comes from a story in which all the superheroes Josh had ever heard of combine forces to capture the Incredible Hulk:

Now there glowed a little light in the sky
and then (it) down came Superman
and he said that Batman wasn't feeling well
(so) 'Well' said Spiderman 'What shall we do
then if Batman isn't well?

Robin's got a chest-ache
and Batman's got flu
well what shall we do now?
(um- we haven't) now what shall we do?
we never can get help'
'I don't know'
but again (but that-but) that stupid Spiderman fell
in the river again
so they have to (go) pull him out more
well the only one who could it wasn't Batman
it wasn't Robin
it wasn't Spiderman
and it was Superman who done it
he pulled him out of that disgusting water

In this extract Josh combines the narrator's telling with the characters' showing, through their dialogue, what the problem of the story is. As in the last passage the unidentified narrator's voice is clearly heard in the 'Now' which opens the quotation, and in the thrice repeated 'It wasn't' clauses which lead up to Superman's rescue of Spiderman. The narrator's stance to the events narrated can also be heard in 'stupid' and 'disgusting'. Though the hidden narrator is still present and firmly in control of the telling, Josh also lets the characters, through their questions and responses, state both the story's problem and the reason why there is a problem.

In Josh's earlier stories, told at the beginning of his storytelling year, dialogue tends to be brief, as it is in the superheroes story. But as his storytelling develops so the conversations held by his characters become more extended, taking over many of the narrator's functions – giving information, hypothesizing about what might happen, supplying explanations and reasons, and coming to agreements, resolutions and conclusions. Josh's characters not only discuss their ideas among themselves, but their ideas and opinions establish what kinds of character they are. Through the consistency of their behaviour, reported largely through what they say, Josh's characters create a plot.

In a long story called 'The God Fairy', told in three chapters six months into his storytelling year, Josh's developing skill at representing argument as a dialogue between two characters is very clearly demonstrated. 'The God Fairy' emerged after a period in which Josh had told a series of stories which were similar in length, plot, characters, and in the move from a 'real' world setting to a fantasy world. In his earlier stories the imagined world had occasionally been Heaven, but more often it was a vague other-world of mountains in the clouds, inhabited by witches and fairies and an Oz-like God figure, and strongly reminiscent of the terrain of Baum's Oz stories, which I had been reading aloud to Josh night after night. Josh's characters had been a fictionalized self and his friends, but in 'The God Fairy' the children are transformed to God, St Peter, and a crowd of servants, and the witches become Frankenstein and Dracula. All the characters are mythical and larger than life, which gives Josh the space to explore issues and conflicts that concern him in a disguised, but maximally pleasureable and exciting way. St Peter is derived from a retelling of the Grimm story *How the Moon Began*, while the labyrinthine setting of Heaven almost certainly comes from Theseus and the minotaur, another story Josh heard at the time. If the total story is a metaphor for Josh's inner and outer living, that metaphor is stitched together in a patchwork of other metaphors from various story sources. Yet running through this intricate total image are conversations which resonate with the social discourses of everyday life. Much of the fun of 'The God Fairy' comes from the contrast between the super-powerful roles of the characters, and the very domestic nature of their speech – a technique which adult writers often use in comedy and parody.

Josh's story opening establishes at once that a great deal of the story's content will consist of God and St Peter thrashing out their problems in discussion:

> once in the palace (um) of God St Peter
> walked around a passageway without God
> God was sitting on his throne
> once (um) St Peter went back to God
> he found a clue St Peter did
> it was a little puppy
> 'Oh no    that is somebody's (from-from-from-
> who) who's dead who's just climbed up
> these mountains and just got here'
> 'he's alive'
> 'yes    I don't know what we can do with him'
> 'we'll just (we'll just) throw him back
> down'
> 'don't throw him back down' said St Peter
> 'we must treat him nicely'
> so they didn't throw him down

Here the action is minimal. We have God sitting and St Peter finding a clue. Then the two protagonists take over all the narrating functions, explaining how the puppy got to Heaven in a story time before this narrative begins, and hypothesizing how he can be returned to earth, in a story time which projects forward from the 'present' of God and St Peter's dialogue. Inserting what is effectively verbal role-play into a story produces these narrative time-shifts (see Meek 1984) quite effortlessly. Though the analysis of what Josh does makes it sound complex, as indeed it is, in fact all he is doing is catching the 'tune' of the ways people speak to one another, and he repeats this theme in point/counter-point as a 'rondo' movement throughout his story. The dramatic presentation of the story problems and events has the further advantage of establishing character traits. St Peter throughout is the voice of caution and gentle behaviour, while all the story's major actions, including the violent ones St Peter is afraid of, are performed by God. When I listen to Josh telling this story on the tape I often hear the tones of two adults, perhaps a mother and a father, deciding whether to pursue a particular course of action or not.

There then follows a long explanation from St Peter of how the puppy was able to open the door to God's throne room:

> (um) once the dog was walking along the passage
> ways like this (and then – and then) until he
> found a door
> and he opened the door
> and there was a throne
> and it had God sitting
> 'There he is again'
> 'Yes I wonder how he opened the door?'
> 'I know' (said) said St. Peter
> 'I followed him
> and he climbed up the door (and then) and then
> hanged from the thingy
> and then he jumped down
> and then he pushed (with his) with his head
> until it opened
> and then he came in'
> 'But where were you?'
> 'I came in another way
> but when I saw him when I went across him
> he went that way
> and I went like that
> and then I went like that
> but he went the quickest way'

The quest for *vraisemblance* is a very serious one for all the five children in my study. Even in highly improbable fantasy stories like this one they are concerned to make events as credible and plausible as possible. Explanations, like this one, are given in great detail, so that we should be in no doubt that the storyteller knows what he is talking about. Notice that St Peter's explanation of how a puppy can open a door is still insufficient for God, who wants to know why St Peter, if he was there, didn't simply open the door for the puppy. God is the interrogator of St Peter's text. However, St Peter's explanation is not simply a bit of detailed verisimilitude to pad out the story, for God's response to St Peter's reported narrative moves the story on and returns it to the problem of whether to keep the puppy in Heaven as a useful sort of pet, or whether to return it to its rightful owners on earth:

> 'Oh he's a clever dog
> I think we must have him for something'
> 'Oh don't   the people might want him'
> 'Oh yes' said God 'but there's no way to take him down
> we'll die if we go down

[(*To mother*) will they die if they go (down) down?
*Mother*: Uhum
(*To mother*) (um) God? Will he? Will he really Mum?
*Mother*: Maybe   I don't know]

(so) so we can't take him down'
'the only thing we can do is send one of our
servants down in an aeroplane'
'but they'll die'
'there's no way except to throw him down
I know what
get him in a box and throw him down'
'Oh yes'
they made a box for him
(and there's your) and there's a little hole
for him to look

Note that Josh actually stops the story here to obtain confirmation of the 'facts' of his story. The parents in the study were not usually allowed nor expected to interrupt the children's narrations unless the storytellers themselves wanted some sort of help. The younger children, whose ages were from three-and-a-half to five, sometimes 'dried up' during storytelling, and then their parents would prompt them with a question or suggest how they might continue. But the two five-year-olds *only* stop the narrative to check that their facts are right. To me this confirms that creating an illusion was a serious business for the children, requiring much knowledge of the physical and social world. Indeed, I have reported elsewhere (Fox 1989) that their imaginary worlds are made 'real' by recourse to what are the beginnings of non-narrative discourses – science and mathematics, for example, in the spatial and temporal aspects of their narrating.

To continue 'The God Fairy', the puppy is now returned to the roof of his own house, throws the box back up to Heaven, and God and St Peter celebrate by dancing around with the servants until bedtime. In the night Dracula creeps through the passageways, but is promptly despatched by God, who stabs him with his own fangs and buries him with no tombstone. At this point Frankenstein pays God a visit:

(and then- and then) and then somebody else
came in
(and it was) and it was Frankenstein
and then Frankenstein said 'Hey God?'
'What?'
'Dracula – where's Dracula?'
'Oh he's buried'
'How?'
(um-er) 'I'm sorry to tell you but he's buried'
'Oh good   I didn't like Dracula very much did you?'
'No   he's dead now'
'I think he's thirty-six'

'Oh he couldn't be that many'
'He could be about a hundred and one'
'Oh yes that's how many he is'
'oh he must be dead'
'yeah I stabbed him with one of my teeth' said God
'I pulled (one o his) one o his teeth out and
stabbed him with it
and then he died'
'Where did you stab him?'
'Right in the heart and the (teeth) tooth came
right out of (his) the back of his heart on his back'
'Oh that's good
so now he's dead is he?
Oh oh' said Frankenstein 'I've just got (some) some
good news to tell you
There's a dragon (who) who's very kind
and if he comes in don't be scared of him and try to
kill him
he's nice'

This dialogue is full of the phatic markers of a conversation between two people who are familiar with one another rather than really close – the frequent use of 'Oh' for example to express surprise or, more frequently, agreement. The whole conversation seems to be about the establishment of a consensus between Frankenstein and God that Dracula deserved his fate. We might expect Frankenstein to be at least as bad a 'baddie' as Dracula, and the implication at the beginning of the conversation is that Frankenstein has come looking for his old pal, but the impact of God's cautionary narrative of Dracula's death is sufficient to ward off any danger Frankenstein might have been expected to pose. God keeps the real story of what happened to Dracula until the end of the conversation; it is elicited as a result of Frankenstein's constant questioning, which at first produces only the elliptic 'Oh he's buried' from God. In this dialogue Josh is able to give a more detailed and extended account of Dracula's death, which earlier in the story had been reported very briefly and concisely. The conversation also further underlines God's mastery of events since he is the character with the power to reveal or conceal in this conversation, a metaphor for the mastery of the storyteller. I often wonder about the fortuitous nature of this part of the story, for Josh did not consciously think out its structure in the way that could be implied by my reading of it. There was no time for that. He tells the story breathlessly, as if the words could not keep up with the images in his head. But as he tells it it is clear that he is totally imaginatively immersed in what is happening. The consistency of his characters and themes and the unity of the structures in the story are a reflection of a concentrated 'indwelling' in the story. As he tells, *all points of view are in his mind.* The very activity of verbal role-play creates an argument for him, as each speech or question demands a response from the addressee, which calls forth another response and keeps the conversation going. It is this which seems to me to have such important implications for narrative as the vessel which can carry, lightly and naturally, the weight of reasoned argument.

Like the messenger in Greek tragedies, Frankenstein is the bringer of news – a final visitor to Heaven, a 'kind dragon', who in fact returns us to the puppy theme of the opening episode:

> one night a dragon came in
> (and they said   and he said   and) but St Peter
> said to God 'Don't kill him
> (remember what) remember what he said'
> and the dragon came near him and said 'What
> is your command?'
> and he said 'We don't have any commands
> Can you be our pet?' says God
> 'Of course I can'
> so (they kept him in-in a-in-in a big) they put
> him to sleep in a big bag
> they just left a little hole in it (for for) for
> him to breathe
> and when it's morning they took him out for any
> dangers
> (and) and one night (um) a danger happened
> Dracula had came alive again
> he had had his teeth in again by a special
> dentist underground who was magic
> so the dragon caught him and put fire to him
> he never came alive again
> (and) and that's the end

Dracula's rebirth may seem to be a bit of convenient magic here, but notice how carefully it is explained, argued even, as at least a possibility given the evidence which Josh supplies. Having established Dracula's ability to appear and reappear in the narrative, and the problem this poses for God and St Peter, the scene is set for the second chapter, in which God and St Peter, again in conversation, are forced to resolve the problem of his evil by turning him into a friend.

There is a sense in which 'The God Fairy' is a metaphor for Josh's own storytelling, or the act of narration itself. During this period of his life storytelling and listening to stories occupied a considerable part of his free time. In his storytelling Josh wants to have fun, to be daring and exciting, to deal with what is usually forbidden, to go 'over the top'. However, the conventions of narration constrain him to tell what is fictionally credible, explicable and rational. The puppy and the dragon must be able to breathe in the box which is thrown down to earth and the bag which is put into the bed. The threat of Frankenstein must be neutralized (*by a story*), and Dracula must be converted to God's side. Those who remain in the palace of God must be his friends. Narrative discourse constrains Josh to impose order on what is disorderly and rude, just as Abrahams (1972,

p. 238), in his account of 'talking broad' in St Vincent, claims that the rules of verbal play constrain the players in this Caribbean form of verbal duelling.

Vygotsky (1978, pp. 101–3) has claimed that the imaginative situation, which he sees as play's defining characteristic, makes play 'a means of developing abstract thought' and therefore 'a leading factor in development'. In the same passage he suggests that in play 'a child always behaves above his average age, above his daily behaviour'. It may be true that for a lot of the time in ordinary life children find it difficult to see viewpoints other than their own, and are not yet highly developed reasoners, explicators, or rational debaters. But in the context of a familiar set of discourses, those of fantasy storytelling, which on the face of it might be the last areas we would investigate to discover the more rational aspects of their thinking, they sometimes show, embedded in the pleasure and excitement of their 'yarning on', cool and serious minds at work, weighing up the pros and cons of imaginary problems, problems posed by themselves as narrators, and solved in satisfying and elegant ways. When Dracula finally reforms his character at the end of Josh's second chapter he knows that he must now tell God and St Peter a new story about himself:

> 'well once I'll tell you the life that I had
> on earth once
> once somebody tried to get me
> I didn't suck anybody's blood
> I'm a good Dracula'

Perhaps a story is an argument after all.

# 4 Learning to control different written registers

BRIAN CAMBOURNE AND
HAZEL BROWN

## The problem

We believe that one major outcome of successful literacy teaching ought to be the ability to control a wide range of linguistic registers. By 'registers' we mean types of oral and written discourse which serve specific functions. A sermon, a joke, a debate, a plenary session at a conference, are all examples of oral registers which have a specific linguistic function. They also have a characteristic linguistic organization which in part serves to define this function. Thus if the form of discourse we know as 'the joke' is to retain its 'joke-ness' (or any other other register its 'debate-ness', 'sermon-ness', or 'plenary session-ness') then it will need to follow a certain predictable pattern.

There are also written registers which have specific organizational characteristics. Narrative in all its diverse forms (adventure, fairy tale, myth, legend, science fiction, etc.) is one. Then there are factual registers, such as, procedure, recount, report, explanation, exposition (i.e. argument), and so on. The organization of narrative is different from that of report, which is different from that of a recount, which differs from exposition.

By 'control of a register' we mean the ability to read and write independently in that individual register. This entails not only being aware of what the organizational shape of any form of discourse is, but also being able to bring into play the thinking and 'language-ing' processes that have to go into the production of a text that conforms to a specific register's conventional organizational 'shape'.[1]

We also believe that those who have acquired control over the registers which their culture values are able to exert more control over their lives within that culture than those who have not. Furthermore, the links between language and thought suggest that those who have gained control (as we define it) over a wide range of diverse registers are better equipped to think in diverse ways.

This is especially true of the academic registers which schools and universities expect to be learned and used. If one is to understand and succeed in the different subjects which are taught in schools and universities one must learn to think like a historian, economist, literary critic, biologist, mathematician, or whatever. In order to do this one must learn not only the content of these discipline areas, but also the ways of organizing the discourse that typifies them. Students are expected to be able to both read and write the various forms of narrative and factual texts if they are to succeed academically. As teachers of literacy we are expected to help our learners gain control over these registers. Herein lies the problem: how are registers learned? How can they be taught in schools?

In order to illuminate this question let us examine a case of what we consider to be an example of the successful acquisition of two different written registers.

## The case of Peter

As stated above, control of a register seems to have got something to do with being able to read and write in that register independently. Peter, a Year 5 child, is a case in point. Peter wrote both the texts reproduced below within a month of each other. Both grew out of a theme of 'Arctic animals' his class had been studying.[2] At the same time his reading log showed that he had read and discussed a number of texts which were exemplars of the registers being studied.

### Lemmings

Lemmings are small furry animals that look like hamsters. They live in the Arctic. Lemmings do not hibernate or turn white in winter. A female lemming can produce eight litters of five or six a year. Because of its rapid reproduction most animals are not getting enough food, so they have to move across the tundra. Most lemmings are eaten by snowy owls, arctic foxes or wolves, and many die crossing the rivers. When summer comes lemmings store food in their burrows to eat in winter. When winter comes lemmings are safe underground and are well fed with grasses and other plants. If a lemming should decide to come out it will freeze very quickly, unless a predator spots it first.

### The tale of Leppy the lemming

Far, far away in the Arctic Circle in a small burrow under the snow lived Leppy the lemming. Winter was nearly over and Leppy, his five sisters, and his mother were waiting for the first signs of spring so that they could leave their burrow and begin eating the fresh spring grass which would soon be on the tundra. It was time for them to leave the safety of their burrow and move out on their own to begin their families.

At last the day came. But alas, as Mother lemming cautiously left the burrow, sniffing the air cautiously a large arctic owl swooped down and almost caught her and carried her off. She rushed back down the burrow and told Leppy and his sisters that they could not leave just yet as it was too dangerous. They were trapped, and would soon starve unless they could get out and feed on the fresh spring grass. They had to work out a way to escape the clutches of the owl.

Leppy had an idea. He took his mother's sewing kit and one of her old dresses and sewed and sewed all night. In the morning he had made a look-alike lemming by stuffing the clothes he had sewn with some of the grass and roots their mother had stored from her collecting and gathering last summer. At first light they threw it out on to the space at the front of their burrow. The owl swooped and was away with the dummy before you could give two hoots. Before it realised that it had been tricked Leppy and his family were free and safe, ready to feed on the summer pastures. Leppy and his family lived happily ever after.

Peter's first text displays many of the organizational criteria and linguistic characteristics which identify the form of discourse known as 'report'. According to Martin and Rothery (1981a) a report has the following features:

- it deals with factual information;
- it focuses on a group or class of things rather than an individual;
- it may describe an experience or report on the information that has been gathered;
- it has a *general introduction* to the thing to be talked about which is followed by *descriptions* of specific aspects of the subject;
- it may also contain generalizations, classifications and/or explanations; and
- the writer does not make any personal comment.

On the other hand, Peter's second text displays many of the organizational criteria and linguistic forms which are characteristic of the textual form known as the narrative. According to Martin and Rothery (1981a) a narrative has the following features:

- an orientation sets the scene and introduces the main characters;
- something happens – a complication;
- resolution – the complication is resolved;
- a number of different complications and resolutions may occur in the one narrative; and
- a coda, or a comment on the story as a whole, may be tacked onto the end.

Peter's decision to write both a report and a narrative about what was essentially the same content involved him in some very nimble linguistic foot-work. In the process of writing each piece he had to delve into his pool of linguistic knowledge to find at least two kinds of information: that which related to the organization of each piece and that pertaining to the sounds, words and syntactic options he had available which would best support this organization.

His choice of words and his way of organizing them for each piece seem to us to be appropriate. It seems appropriate for example that a narrative (a fairy tale in this case) should begin with words like 'Far, far away in . . .' and not a factual statement such as 'Lemmings are small furry animals . . .'. 'Once upon a time' would have been an alternative acceptable way of beginning his fairy tale. As we read through Peter's fairy tale we were aware that the majority of Peter's choices seemed to be appropriate. Our linguistic intuitions led us to expect a fairy tale to contain phrases like 'It was time for . . .' and 'At last the day came', 'At first light . . .', 'But alas . . .', 'sewed and sewed'. We also expected it to be in the past tense. We expected it to entertain or amuse. In other words his piece seemed to us to fulfil most of the conventions we have come to associate with the narrative form we know as the 'fairy tale'.

On the other hand, his report uses quite different sorts of words, organized in quite different ways, which again seem to be appropriate. Reports are expected to contain words like 'hibernate' rather than 'sleep', 'female lemming' rather than 'mother lemming', 'litter' rather than 'five sisters' or 'family'. Reports are expected to use the present tense. Reports are expected to begin with statements which introduce the topic, rather than the setting. Reports are expected to flesh out the details of whatever the topic is. Reports are expected to inform and explain.

What is it that Peter must have known in order to make these kinds of linguistic choice? We would argue that at the very least he needed to be either intuitively or consciously aware of the following:

- The relationship between purpose, word choice, and textual organization. In this particular case he needed to be aware that written texts which set out to amuse or entertain (e.g. fairy tales), are different, both with respect to word choice and structural organization, from texts which set out to inform or explain (e.g. reports).
- The link between textual organization and the relationship one has with the intended audience of the text. For example the language one uses to entertain or inform a close relative or acquaintance is different from that which would be used to entertain and/or inform an audience at a conference of academic peers whom one has never met.

In other words, in order to write his report and his narrative Peter had to be capable of some complicated linguistic decision-making. Not only did he need to have a large pool of linguistic knowledge somewhere inside his head, but he had to be able to make some sophisticated choices from within that pool. When we interviewed him about these two pieces he informed us that in each piece the female lemming was, in his mind, the same one, and that the 'litter of five or six' in the report was really 'Leppy and his five sisters' in the 'story' (i.e. narrative). In other words because of the decisions he made about purpose and audience, and because of the implicit and explicit knowledge he had about the linguistic expectations that such choices entailed, he had been constrained to select different sets of words to refer to what were essentially (in his mind at least) the same real world objects, and to organize these words in ways that were appropriate for the purposes he had in mind.

As well as such linguistic prowess we would argue that Peter also needed what we have loosely called 'process knowledge', that is, he needed to be familiar with the processes that underpin effective writing. He needed to know how to draft, revise, edit, find information, shape it, seek responses to his evolving meanings, deal with blockages, and a whole set of heuristics which effective writers can bring to bear as they work towards a final written product.

The question is, of course, how do learner-writers like Peter get all the knowledge of language, language forms, and processes which enable them to make the appropriate linguistic choices? This is another way of asking how we can help young learner-writers acquire control of different registers. This is what we shall address in the next section.

## How can we help young learner-writers get control of different registers?

Peter was one of many children in one Year 5 class who were observed to be making steady and regular gains in their control of a variety of registers. In a few months the majority of them had gained strong control over a number of forms of narrative (fairy tale, fable, myth, legend), as well as report, description, and persuasion (i.e. argument). This success had been repeated by the teacher with other grades over a three-year period.

In what follows we shall attempt to clarify the links between classroom teaching activities and the learning of different registers. We shall synthesize (and thus oversimplify) the results of an ongoing three-year longitudinal study of one teacher's classroom, during which time she taught two Year 5 and one Year 3 class. The study was naturalistic in orientation and based on a 'teacher-as-co-researcher' model of co-operative research (Cambourne and Turbill 1988). This means that both university researcher (Cambourne) and classroom teacher (Brown) have been participant-observers in the learning of the children who had been members of the various class groups which were taught. Over the years a range of data has been collected, including handwritten observations of language lessons ('specimen records'); over 100 hours of transcribed video- and audio-tape records of the ongoing classroom behaviours; written artefacts (teacher records and plans, children's written products); records of interviews between researcher and teacher, researcher and children, and teacher and children; and records of interviews/discussions between the co-researchers after viewing and reading the data ('retrospective debriefing sessions').

*Teaching/learning procedures*

An analysis of the teaching/learning behaviours which preceded the acquisition of different textual forms by pupils like Peter shows that the processes involved each time were highly similar. What follows is a brief descriptive summary of the nature of the teaching/learning events that surrounded the acquisition of each text form. If the context or theme which the teacher generated lent itself to the exploration of a particular linguistic register such as 'report', or 'argument' or 'narrative', then the teacher used a common strategy and set of tactics to help the learners gain control of the register. Typically this sequence of activities took place over a two- to three-week span, and involved two hours each day.

Figure 4.1 is a schematic representation which tries to encapsulate the flow of activities associated with the treatment of each register. It flows roughly from top to bottom. As it shows, the overarching teaching strategy is one of *immersion*. The teacher uses a range of tactics to immerse ('saturate', 'steep', 'bathe', 'surround') the learners in the register she has chosen to focus on. While the tactics which can be brought into play to achieve immersion are many and varied, this teacher used a total of six, namely *demonstration, response, individual reading, sharing/discussion, retelling, writing independently, generating criteria*. As Figure 4.1 shows, some of these were co-requisites in that they generally occurred side by side and tended to support each other (demonstration, response, individual reading, sharing/ discussion, retelling). On the other hand, these were prerequisites of others: writing independently depended on these four and was in turn a prerequisite for generating criteria. In other words 'writing independently' and 'generating criteria' were tactics which we employed after the other four had been in operation for some time.

Because the six immersion tactics/strategies used in this classroom overlapped and supported each other they are difficult to describe as discrete entities. The best we can do is to describe how they were manifested in teacher and learner behaviours.

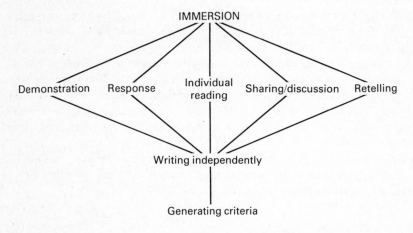

*Figure 4.1:*   Classroom tactics used in acquiring control of registers

*How the immersion tactics were used*

The teacher used the first fifteen to twenty-five minutes of her daily language session to read a selection of examples of whichever register was being treated at the time. Thus when she was treating fable she used this time to read many fables. When she was treating report she read many examples of reports, which were relevant to some content theme being treated (e.g. 'Rainforests'). When she was treating argument (i.e. persuasive texts) she read as many examples of them as possible (e.g. letters to the editor, anti-smoking literature, conservation literature). In this first period she might read between three and five samples of the particular register which lent itself to the theme being treated (*demonstration*).

This was always followed by a period of up to twenty minutes of independent reading which was called 'sustained silent reading' (SSR). In SSR time children were encouraged to read other examples of whatever register was the focus at the time. This meant that the teacher had to both make available samples of whatever form of discourse was the focus at the time, and create meaningful reasons for the children to want to select and read these samples during this period of time (*demonstration, individual reading*).

The teacher demonstrated the process by thinking out loud as she did things. For example she might say something like: 'I'm going to show you how I write the first draft of a persuasive or argumentative piece of text. I'm going to do it on the overhead projector so that you can all see, and as I do it I'll think out loud so you know what's going on inside my head.' This kind of 'think-aloud' demonstration was repeated for such processes as revising, editing, finding information, getting over writer's block (and reader's block), and a wide variety of other procedural and strategic aspects of reading and writing (*demonstration*).

Each reading of different types of text by the teacher was followed by discussion which she initiated and led. Her comments and questions were ones which focused the children's attention on what she considered to be the salient features of the particular written register being used. Thus she might ask the learners to speculate on the purposes which each written register might serve, or on the relationship that the author was trying to establish with the reader, or on the similarities and/or differences between different examples of the same register. Then again she might focus the children on aspects of the processes which the author might have used to achieve the purposes which they had identified. In such discussion periods she might raise questions of how the authors (Aesop and La Fontaine when dealing with fable, or a range of journalists or writers when dealing with persuasion) might have set about the task of writing such pieces. Such discussion could range over such things as where the authors might have got their ideas, how they made decisions about purpose and audience, how such pieces might have been drafted, how they eventually were put into final form, whether they were meant to be told or read, and so on (*response, demonstration, sharing/discussion*).

As part of a four-weekly 'language contract' the children were expected to use what she called 'elective activity time' (about one hour per day) to choose from a range of language activities. Some of these activities involved preparing, drafting, revising, and ultimately getting ready for 'publication' some pieces of 'quality' writing, including examples of whichever form was being treated. During this period the teacher constantly 'roved', interacting with children about their tasks and responding to their requests for assistance and/or clarification. During this time also the learners were free to interact with each other and to help each other complete whatever reading and writing tasks had to be done (*demonstration, response, sharing/discussion, writing independently*).

During a part of the daily language session called 'elective activity time' the teacher peeled off a different group of six children from the main body for a compulsory activity which she called 'retelling procedure' (Brown and Cambourne 1987). Each child would engage in retelling procedure about once per fortnight. Retelling procedure is a teaching/learning activity which involves the children in the group making some written predictions about a previously unseen text's storyline (if a narrative) or possible content (if factual) on the basis of the title. These predictions are then shared and discussed within the group. They then hear the text read, and then read it silently themselves any number of times before going to a quiet corner of the room to attempt to retell it in writing for someone who has not previously read or heard it. Finally, this group shares its retellings and compares them in terms of content, structure, paraphrase, use of words and phrases, or any aspect of text, language, or process which the teacher thinks is of interest or value. This activity typically engages this group for thirty to forty minutes, with the teacher returning to them when discussions need to be initiated or monitored (*retelling, response, demonstration, individual reading, sharing/discussion*).

The last fifteen minutes of each language session was called 'sharing time'. In sharing time learners volunteer to share what they read during SSR time, or drafts of what they wrote during elective activity time. Typically they are questioned by the rest of the group about what they share. During the fable period of the programme many of the sharings were based on fables which had been read and/or were being written. A similar context was created when argumentative texts were being treated (*sharing/discussion, demonstration, response*).

When all had finished their contracted pieces of 'quality' writing, class charts which summarized the criteria which the children thought distinguished each form were developed from class and group discussions and displayed as references to assist with future writing tasks (*generating criteria, response, sharing/discussion*). Figure 4.2 is an example of three such criteria charts.

### Is this all there is to it?

Our data strongly suggest that the learning context in this classroom was much more complex than a mere description of strategies and tactics would suggest. Other less tangible, subtle, yet we believe, related factors, have begun to emerge from the data as we continue to analyse them. Here are some which we believe are important:

### There was a very strong 'pro-reading/pro-writing' ethos permeating the whole class

Our interview data and our observational data revealed very clearly that the majority of children in these classes believed that reading and writing were extremely important activities which were not only worth engaging with but which were also worth learning to control. Our data indicated that these beliefs could

## REPORT CRITERIA

- Contains true information.
- Begins with a statement which tells you about the topic (this is the equivalent of 'Once upon a time').
- Often has sub-headings which categorize the information. This helps:
  (a) the reader to find information.
  (b) the writer to organize his thoughts.
- Often about places, animals or what has happened.
- Reports have no obvious ending; you can add or subtract information without spoiling it.
- Uses scientific language, rather than imaginative language (similes, etc.).
- Concentrates on one major theme, e.g. bees. Stories weave bits and pieces together.
- Most reports are written in the present tense. Reports cannot be written in the future tense because reports have to contain true information. They are occasionally written in the past tense.


## CHART SUMMARIES MADE BY CLASS

*What is a fairytale?*
1 Usually about princes and princesses.
2 Leads and endings are similar:
  'Once upon a time . . .'
  'They lived happily ever after'.
3 Lots of magic and fantasy.
4 Animals turn into princes.
5 Tales are told in 3rd person.
6 Fairytales sometimes teach a lesson.

*What makes a fable a fable?*
1 Always has a moral or lesson at end.
2 It is always short in length.
3 Usually contains animals of different species.
4 Animals act and talk like humans.
5 Many of our sayings come from fables:
  - slow and steady wins the race – Tortoise and Hare
  - look before you leap – Goat and Frogs
  - be thankful for what you've got – Goose and Golden Eggs
  - never try to be someone else.

*Figure 4.2:*   Criteria charts generated by learners

not be attributed to home background, but were a function of the learning contexts which the teacher deliberately and consciously established. However, the processes by which she established these contexts were ubiquitous in that we cannot describe them as a set of discrete, linear steps. Rather they seem to be part of an aggregate of such things as:

*The way she used language*: she used language which invited and encouraged participation in, and speculation about, the use of both oral and written language more often than she used language which managed and directed.

*The expectations she communicated*: she repeatedly communicated the message that reading and writing were worth mastering, that each one of the class members was capable of mastering them, that control led to empowerment as learners and that she genuinely cared for and valued each one of her pupils as learners and people.

*Her practice of making explicit what she valued with respect to literature*: she continually shared her enthusiasms and dislikes with respect to literature, writers and writing.

*Her practice of making explicit the connections between process and product*: she continually modelled the connections she had made between reading, writing and learning, as well as the connections between registers. ('Here's how I get over writer's block . . .', 'This is how I think I learn to spell . . . if you continually read and write the words seem to stick with you . . .', 'Here's how I think a good persuasive piece of writing is organized . . . what do you think?')

*Her practice of encouraging approximation*: she insisted that learners should first 'have a go' at solving reading/writing tasks using their own underdeveloped literacy knowledge/skill before seeking assistance from a more knowledgeable source. Thus learners would attempt to write an argumentative text before studying how such texts were structured, or asking someone how to do it, etc. Sensible, logical approximations were celebrated and reflected upon.

*Her practice of encouraging reflection*: reflecting on the processes and knowledge one had drawn upon to solve a literacy-related task (e.g. writing argument) was an expected and regular activity, either in the form of oral discussions in groups or in the form of reflective journals which were also shared (*response, retelling, sharing/discussion*). One of the major purposes of these activities was to raise each learner's conscious awareness[3] of text structure and of the processes which can be used to construct it.

*Her practice of emphasizing the social dimensions of learning*: she continually communicated the expectation that reading/writing problems were best resolved by engaging in discussions with peers first before seeking her help.

*Her insistence on justification*: she also created the expectation that statements about texts, books, authors should always be justified. Thus, one wouldn't be allowed to respond to a question, 'What did you think of *The Lion, the Witch and the Wardrobe*?' with a simple 'It was good (or bad)'. Rather one would be expected to justify one's opinion with a 'because' statement followed by examples from the text.

*Her practice of careful, deliberate, but subtle intervention*: When dealing with each register the teacher constantly intervened in the learning. Two broad types of intervention emerged from the data. The first was intervention at the whole-class level. The teacher not only chose the models in which she would immerse the learners, but she engaged in a form of teacher behaviour which we have called 'raising the salience of features of demonstrations'. By this we mean that she focused the learners' attention on the salient features of any demonstration she supplied. She did this in a number of ways, including: carefully chosen questions ('How is a fable different from a fairy tale?', 'What kinds of words help us persuade readers of our point of view?'); constant recapping and summarizing during discussions ('Let me see if we can pull together the main points of what we've discovered about writing an argumentative text'); and 'hit-and-run-never-let-a-chance-go-by' demonstrations ('Stop what you're doing and listen to the persuasive piece that Leminh's just drafted. I think it's a good one because . . . Now get back on with what you were doing'). The second type of intervention occurred at the individual level. During interactions with individual children the teacher used all of the intervention behaviours described above. She also engaged in a form of behaviour which has been described as 'applying the ratchet' (Geekie and Keeble 1987). This was related to the expectations she developed about individual children. Our debriefing sessions have identified two levels of expectation. At the global level there was the expectation that reading and writing would be engaged in and learned by each child in the class. At the individual level specific expectations for each child emerged as the teacher learned more about each member of the class. Once she established what she could reasonably expect from each child, she held the child to that level. When the child advanced she held him or her to the new level, by 'applying the ratchet' in much the same way that a fisherman would when reeling in a heavy fish on a fishing rod. Thus when Todd produced something which Cambourne (the observer) thought was of a relatively high standard, Brown (the teacher) berated Todd thus: 'That's not good enough, Todd. I know you can do better.' In almost the same breath she accepted something which Cambourne judged to be of much lesser quality from Jesse, for whom she held quite different expectations. These kinds of global and individual intervention continually permeated the discourse of the classroom.

*There was a high degree of confidence among the learner-writers in the class*

The majority of children in these classes not only believed that they were capable of coping with most of the reading/writing tasks which confronted them, but they fully expected to be able to learn and cope with future reading/writing tasks. Our data indicate that the teacher's willingness to accept approximations to ideal forms and the kinds of expectation she continually communicated were crucial factors in creating this confidence.

## A grounded theory of register acquisition

A 'grounded' theory is one which is 'anchored' or 'grounded' in contextually relevant data. Our data support the following theory of acquisition of different kinds of written register by young learners. Learners will acquire whatever registers teachers value, if they are genuinely convinced that acquisition of such forms of discourse will actually further the purposes of their lives. When a classroom ethos such as that described above is established the probability that learners will engage with the demonstrations of what these text forms look like, what purposes they serve, how they are structured, and how they are written will be maximized. Furthermore, if they are encouraged to 'have a go' ('approximate') and can have their approximations received and commented on in ways which encourage further learning, and which supply more of the information necessary to achieve control, inaccuracies will be dropped from their repertoires and be replaced by more correct versions of the forms they are working with. If they can be helped to reflect upon the processes and knowledge that they are using and make connections between them, through interacting with others, the probability that they will learn the forms will be further maximized.

## Notes

1 One of us (Brown) has coined the term 'authorcraft' to describe this activity. It means more than the mere 'crafting' of a piece of writing through the revising and shaping process. It includes the processes which precede the crafting phase, for example reading and mining other written texts for a wide range of linguistic information which can be used to craft into a written product of some kind.
2 Peter's spelling and punctuation have been tidied up for the purpose of this chapter.
3 We have referred to this elsewhere as 'meta-textual' awareness: see Brown and Cambourne (1987).

# 5 Arguing

IAN FROWE

Given the amount of time and energy that many children expend on arguing, one might expect them to be pretty good at it. However, just as writing stories does not make everyone a Jane Austen, numerous slanging matches do not lead to Socratic dialogues. The ability to argue in a coherent way is as much a learnt skill as throwing clay pots or solving quadratic equations. What passes for 'argument' is often no more than the declaration of opinions embellished with a vigorous trade in personal insults. The inability of many children to follow, construct or analyse arguments stems not from any lack of intellectual capacity but from their probably never having been taught in any systematic way how to do so. The academic study of argument is ancient and yet it is largely ignored in schools. This is a strange omission from the curriculum, for the study and practise of arguing, both orally and in prose, provides opportunities for the development of abilities both analytic and creative. The cognitive aptitudes fostered are also, I would maintain, as near to possessing universal application as is possible, having pertinence to any area where the interchange of ideas, information, values and beliefs occurs.

In this chapter I outline work done with a class of twenty-five top juniors (aged 10–11) of mixed ability on the topic of argumentation. Inevitably some of the finer points of logical thought are ignored or glossed over in order to keep the work enjoyable and accessible to the children.

## Giving reasons

Central to arguing is the giving of reasons in order to support a particular point of view. Reasons can, however, be 'good reasons' or 'bad reasons' and if we wish to argue well we need to distinguish between the two. A suitable starting point and a way of gaining some insight into the degree of argumentative sophistication the children possess is to ask them to evaluate certain reasons given in support of some belief.

The first exercise consisted of imagining an event and then evaluating the reasons given to explain why the event had occurred. A simple four-point scale of evaluation was adopted:[1]

(a)  impossible – this could never be the reason
(b)  possible – this could be a reason but is unlikely
(c)  probable – this could be a reason and seems likely
(d)  conclusive – this *is* the reason

So:
*Event*: The car will not start

*Reasons*:
1  It's Friday
2  There is no petrol in the tank
3  The car is tired
4  The car is being obstinate
5  The battery is flat

This seemingly simple exercise produced much heated debate. Several children took (3) as being a possible reason for the car's failure to start, much to the amusement of others who rejected it as impossible. The way those who accepted (3) as a possibility defended their position was highly illuminating and showed strong elements of anthropomorphism. The numerous early reading books which portray inanimate objects as possessors of human traits had obviously had a lasting effect on the psyche of some children!

Reason (4) was rejected by the vast majority of children, even some of those who had been willing to accept (3) as a possibility. Why 'obstinacy' should be thought less likely than 'tiredness' for those who accepted the latter was not clear. To accept (3) or (4) as possible reasons is a 'category mistake'; it is an example of confusion over the legitimate ascription of dispositions to types of objects. Eventually, after much discussion, those who had been inclined to give credence to (3) or (4) came round to seeing that their choice had been mistaken.

Reason (1) also caused disagreement as some children tried to invent scenarios that would make the day of the week a possible explanation. What they did was to introduce *something else* as the real reason but related to a certain day of the week, for example 'my dad doesn't get paid until Friday and has no money to buy petrol', or 'if it was very cold or wet the car might not start'. What these responses revealed was considerable confusion as to what was being proposed as a possible explanation, namely the *actual day* of the week, not events which may, as a matter of fact, have occurred on that day. When the issue was pursued many children found it extremely difficult to express clearly why the day of the week could not be considered as a possible reason for the car's failure to start. Many had an intuitive feeling that it was impossible, but lacked the ability to express their reasons unambiguously. Eventually one of the brightest children, after considerable thought, said, 'It's just that days of the week aren't the sort of things that can make things happen'. This conceptual breakthrough about the nature of causality, which to some adults may seem trivial, came as a flash of light to many of the class who had been groping in the dark.[2]

Reasons (2) and (5) were generally agreed upon as being the most likely reasons for the car's reluctance to jump into life, but some children were adamant in picking *one* of them as conclusive. Opting for one in favour of the other was usually because of personal experience: 'Our car wouldn't start last week and it *was* because the battery was flat'. The rejoinder 'Yes, but it *could* have been something else' was countered with 'But it wasn't something else, it was the battery' and details of looking for spanners, taking out the battery, recharging and subsequent successful starting of the car were brought in to support the case.

The idea that there may be more than one possible reason for an event was readily accepted by some children, but others were keen to choose one reason and stick to it as if the illusion of 'certainty', however ill-founded, was preferable to a state of 'not knowing'.

Reasons for believing that the earth is flat or round provide scope for discussion:

*The world is flat*
*Reasons*:
1 If it wasn't flat everyone would fall over
2 People used to believe you could fall off the edge
3 People in Australia would be upsidedown if it wasn't
4 It looks flat

*The world is round*
*Reasons*:
1 In comics it's drawn round
2 You can go round it and come back to where you started
3 My dad told me it's round
4 Photographs from space show it to be round

Encouraging children to add their own reasons, good or bad, for each belief will develop their argumentative abilities and enable them to gain an insight into the different ways in which beliefs are established and maintained.

As a way of approaching the subject of arguing these types of exercise proved to be useful. First, they gave a good insight to the levels of argumentative ability within the class. Second, and perhaps crucially, they provided the children with the opportunity to clarify their own ideas by examining the principles and presuppositions they employ in their own thinking. Latent misguided habits of mind, when brought to the surface, can be properly scrutinized. Third, the ability to evaluate competing reasons is vitally important for the framing of coherent arguments and should not be assumed. Practical work is necessary to get the points across.

**What follows . . . : making inferences**

Argumentative competence involves not only being able to distinguish good from bad reasons but also the ability to work out 'what follows' from a given statement. The 'unpacking' of a statement can be introduced by taking, for example, a triangle.

What follows from 'This shape is a triangle'?

1  It is blue
2  It has three sides
3  It is not a square
4  It is equilateral
5  Its angles will total 180°

The 'unpacking' of the word 'triangle' in terms of valid and invalid inferences encourages clear thinking and an increased awareness of the fact that from one statement it may be possible to establish several others. Again some children were ready to accept (1) or (4) as legitimate inferences on the grounds that 'it *could* be'. Well, yes, it *could* be, but whereas (2), (3) and (5) *must* be the case, (1) and (4) are only *possibilities*. The distinction between inferences that are certain and those which are not needs to be fully discussed, as the drawing of invalid inferences is one of the most common errors in argumentation.

The children can then be set the task of making their own inferences – valid and invalid – from given statements, for example:

(a)  Joey is a goldfish
(b)  It's the 25th December
(c)  Kevin is a football hooligan

There is scope here for amusing as well as logical thought: 'Joey does not take ballet lessons', 'Joey will not be considered for the school football team', for instance. Some inferences are harder to draw than others. In the case of 'Kevin is a football hooligan' what follows was hotly contested. The framing of the inference in a way which did not 'overstep' what could legitimately be extracted was linguistically and intellectually demanding and saw the appearance of qualifications and caveats, e.g. 'Kevin has *probably* been involved in fights', 'On a Saturday Kevin will usually/sometimes go to a football match'. The problem arises, of course, because the notion of a 'hooligan' is more amorphous and complex than, say 'triangle' and therefore demands a more sophisticated treatment. However, it is just such unwieldy concepts that figure in much argument and practice in dealing with them is therefore essential.

From the study of single statements one can move on to simple syllogisms where two statements are used to draw a conclusion:

| | |
|---|---|
| All A are B | All dogs have four legs |
| and A | Bill is a dog |
| Therefore B | Therefore Bill has four legs |

By this time objections such as 'Bill might have been run over and lost one of his legs' were becoming fewer as the children realized that what we were concerned with was not 'Bill the dog' but whether the inference we had drawn actually followed from the two premises. The next step is, of course, to try and catch them out with:

| | |
|---|---|
| All A are B | All dogs have four legs |
| and B | Jeff has four legs |
| Therefore A | Therefore Jeff is a dog |

By now, however, we were on the look-out for bad reasoning and most of the children failed to be duped into drawing the invalid conclusion. Constructing our own syllogisms and testing them on each other became a popular pastime and I extended the work to include arguments of the type:

| | |
|---|---|
| All A are B | All cats are mammals |
| All B are C | All mammals are warm-blooded |
| Therefore all A are C | Therefore all cats are warm-blooded |

Playing around with such syllogisms led to the discovery that a true conclusion could be drawn from false premises. For example:

All children are pigs – false
All pigs have two legs – false
Therefore all children have two legs – true

The inference is valid, although both premises are patently false. Attempts to derive true conclusions from the most outrageously false premises gave free rein to the children's imagination. It is surprising how quickly children can 'tune in' to this sort of work and begin experimenting with various sorts of argument patterns:

All birds have feathers
All feathers can be used for tickling
Therefore all birds can be used for tickling

The discussion raised by such examples provides practice in the analysis and evaluation of arguments.


## Contradictions

How many times do we use the word 'contradiction' or 'contradict' when talking to children? Quite often, but how many can actually explain what a contradiction involves? When I asked my class what a contradiction is and what it means to say that someone has contradicted someone else, the initial reaction was perplexed silence followed by a few tentative suggestions: 'It means to *say* something you shouldn't', 'It means to tell a lie', 'It means to *do* something you shouldn't', 'If you say something horrible about someone that's contradicting them', 'It means to disagree with someone'. Obviously a fair amount of confusion here. The idea that 'contradiction' involves something morally wrong comes, I would suggest, from the reprimand 'Don't you contradict me, young lady/man' when a child is being told off for gainsaying the utterance of an adult. 'Contradicting' is seen as something you have done wrong, such as being insolent.

I then ventured the idea of whether it was possible to contradict yourself. Yes, they had heard people talk about 'contradicting yourself' and this seemed to rule out some of the suggestions already proposed. Many children seemed to have an intuitive notion of what a contradiction was but lacked the vocabulary to express the thought clearly. The idea of 'disagreement' was accepted as an essential part of the concept, but people can disagree about something without contradicting each other. One child then decided to give an example of a contradiction rather than struggle with an abstract definition: 'Mr Jones is a vegetarian and eats meat every day'. So what's a contradiction? 'It's when you say something and then say the opposite' – a fairly reasonable definition. From this we went on to make up our own examples of contradictions: 'This square has five sides', 'The twins have birthdays in May and December', for example. Writing short stories full of contradictions can be a good way of reinforcing the notion. It is important to make the children aware that every form of disagreement is not necessarily a case of contradiction; for example, we may disagree over whether tomato or brown sauce goes best with chips, but it would be inappropriate to describe the situation as a case of contradiction.

## Types of argument

There are several argumentative techniques and it would not be useful or appropriate to try and discuss them all here. However, I chose two well-known forms of argument, one of which I had noticed the children employing in their discussions and another which I thought they might find valuable.

### Ad hominem *arguments*

The underlying idea here is that one's arguments should be consistent, that is, that you should try not to hold conflicting beliefs. Children often show an appreciation of this point by objections in the form, 'Yes, but *you* do/say X'. An argument about hunting brought this out well. One child objected to hunting on the grounds that it was cruel to kill animals. This was immediately seized upon by another who pointed out that the person making this statement had just eaten sausages at lunchtime and the pigs for these had been killed. The point being made is whether someone can maintain that 'killing animals is cruel' and yet eat the products of dead animals. An *ad hominem* argument challenges the consistency of the speaker's beliefs and practices. It may not settle the point at issue, but rather forces scrutiny of the proposer's position.

Reductio ad absurdum *arguments*

This is a more sophisticated technique which proceeds by accepting *for the sake of argument* a particular premise and then drawing out the implication to show that it leads to an unacceptable (absurd?) conclusion. In practice the important point is to encourage the children to listen carefully to their opponents' arguments and look out for any implication that would be considered untenable.

A good example came in a discussion on the problem of house thefts and what could be done to reduce them. One proposal was that all houses should be electrified when empty so that anyone touching any part of the building would receive a severe shock. At first this was thought to be a good solution, until the practical implications of such a system were considered. What about regular callers who deliver milk, mail or read the gas and electricity meters? Oh, they would have 'special keys' to switch the electricity off. But if they had such keys other people could steal them or the people with the keys initially could become burglars. Who precisely would have the keys and would each house have its own key or would one key work on all houses? The impracticality and potential dangers to innocent members of the public soon became clear and the idea was finally rejected for these reasons.

This illustrated well the *reductio* technique of rejecting an argument by initially accepting it and then drawing out its unpalatable implications.

**Using the tools**

> On every side the weeds of error grow;
> Vengeful logician, at them with thy hoe!
> 'Weeding? For that you must not ask!'
> 'Why not?' 'Tool sharpening is my present task'.
> (T. Kotarbinski)

Our work on arguing had been enjoyable and enlightening, not least for the teacher, but the real test was whether we could use our newly developed skills in both the analysis and production of our own arguments? Finding suitable topics for consideration was not difficult, though we decided that there was not much point 'arguing' over something that we all, more or less, agreed about. Subjects on which there was a fair amount of difference of opinion were considered to be far more fertile. We chose three topics for our initial series of debates: capital punishment; UFOs and whether animals should be kept in zoos. Four speakers were selected, two for each side of the argument, and given time to prepare their cases. It was stressed that they should not only concentrate on their own arguments, but think about the arguments their opponents might use both to state their position and to counter theirs. This aspect of preparation – being aware of your opponent's position, both its strengths and weaknesses – is crucial for a good level of debate. The points we had covered were to be held firmly in mind: how good are my arguments? What inferences can be drawn from them? Have I contradicted myself? Am I open to any *ad hominem* or *reductio* arguments and, if so, how will I cope with them?

Those members of the class not acting as speakers in these debates were also encouraged to discuss the issues so that they could contribute to the open forum that would follow the initial interchange. The speakers were given, within reason, as much time as they wanted to prepare their cases. The debates were taped so that we could listen again and see if, with hindsight, there were any points we missed or arguments that could be further discussed. This is useful, as good points often emerge after the discussion has ended, when people have time to think about what has been said.

The debates proved to be extremely interesting and of a very high standard; far higher than what often passes for 'debate' or 'discussion' among adults. The initial set pieces when each side presented its case evidenced much care and thought, but it was the subsequent argument when notes had been forgotten that proved to be the most enjoyable and stimulating. The incisiveness of some of the points and the way positions were defended or adapted to meet objections revealed a depth of intellectual capacity which was quite astounding. The fact that the children had now acquired an 'argument vocabulary' was in no small way a contributing factor here. They had words and phrases with which to organize their ideas and communicate them effectively. 'You can't infer that', 'that doesn't follow', 'that's not consistent with . . .', etc., clearly expressed thought that only a few weeks before we had spent time struggling with due to some degree of linguistic and conceptual confusion. Some of the most incisive points came from children whom one would perhaps not have expected to make them. Many 'quiet' or 'reserved' children overcame their reticence to participate, due to the power of feeling many of the debates engendered. Occasionally other members of the class would watch and listen, partly taken aback by the new light in which certain children were showing themselves. One particularly shy child even gained a spontaneous round of applause!

## Conclusion

As I mentioned at the beginning of this chapter, the study of argument is an ancient discipline but figures little in the primary school curriculum. Whatever the reasons for this – and there are probably several – it cannot be because children of primary school age are not sufficiently developed intellectually to handle the concepts. Young children are probably not going to argue at the level of Kant or Wittgenstein, but neither are they going to produce the mathematics of Euclid, the science of Newton, the literature of Shakespeare or the art of Rembrandt. We do not restrict access to these subjects because of this and should treat argumentation in a similar fashion.

Primary school children are usually eager to learn and are fascinated by new ideas. However, they inhabit a world, along with the rest of us, where every day differing ideas and beliefs are communicated to them through the media: TV, radio, books, magazines, videos, and so on. If they are to make any intelligent judgements on these matters then they need to be equipped with some cognitive framework that enables critical evaluations to be possible.[3] The danger at present is that, although numerous 'policy' and 'curriculum' documents pay lip-service to the inculcation of critical and analytic faculties, precious little is actually done to bring about their realization. Why is this? I offer the following observations.

It has been remarked that 'ideas are dangerous things' and, as we know, Socrates was imprisoned for 'corrupting' the youth of Athens. If we are sincere in our desire to make children questioning and critical we cannot, or should not, be surprised if the recipients of our endeavours begin to bite the hand that feeds them. There may be certain topics that are of a 'sensitive' nature and we may feel inclined to steer clear of them. Now, in some cases there may be justifiable reasons for this: we obviously need to take into account the emotional, social and intellectual maturity of our pupils. However, if we restrict debate on other grounds, such as the wish to uphold religious or political dogma, to protect our own psychological sensibilities or safeguard an authoritarian structure, then we are not involved with education but ideology, and ideology is one of the main enemies of critical thinking. In other words, you cannot have your cake and eat it.

Primary teachers are in a unique position to promote the habits of mind necessary for good argumentative reasoning. Both written and oral work can be developed to encourage the analytic and imaginative capacities of the children. There is also the opportunity to enable considered opinions and beliefs to materialize, resulting in enhanced independence of thought and action.

## Notes

1 Some preliminary discussion of the four terms will be necessary so that everyone is clear about their meaning.
2 The concept of causality is notoriously complex and few children of primary school age will display anything but a superficial understanding. An interesting aspect which can be usefully examined is the difference between natural causal forces, e.g. wind or rain, and the 'causes' of human action.
3 The subject of 'bias' is relevant here. Frowe (1986) outlines one approach to this topic with primary school children.

# 6 A telling story from children's arguments and narratives

## ROSLYN ARNOLD

In reflecting on the theme of this chapter – children's narratives and arguments – I was struck by the irony that, in fact, the kind of rhetoric I am using here may implicitly exemplify the point of view I am proposing. From my own observations and from written texts gathered in a four-year longitudinal study of school-children's writing (Years 6–9 inclusive), I believe that developing writers become increasingly able to draw from 'the universe of discourse' the kinds of rhetoric they need for different purposes. Sometimes one kind alone meets that purpose in one text. Sometimes a melding of forms is required within the one text and an ability to write equally effectively, in, say, narrative and argument, becomes important to meet the writer's intentions.

What happens in real life never exactly matches research paradigms because they are attempts to generalize from experience. We know that generalization involves setting aside the unusual, the ill-fitting or the baffling. And so we categorize different kinds of children's writing according to their most generalizable features, with subsets if necessary. Narrative and argument can be sufficiently different to be recognized as such, but sometimes there is a subtle blending of storytelling and argument to meet the writer's complex need to report, to evaluate, to argue, to reflect. Most experienced readers know whether they have read an argument or a story – just as children know in a social interaction when to produce even an embryonic argument ('All the other children are allowed to go, why can't I?') or a story ('It just fell out of my hand'). What we tend to overlook in our categorizing exercise is the potential affinity between narrative and argument. I would like to explore that further here.

I regard narrative and argument as equally important as part of that rich tapestry of discourse forms we all internalize, along with other experiences and contexts, as we encounter and use language. Common sense tells us that in early childhood children are more commonly reading stories than arguments. However, many childhood stories (fairy tales, parables) have a strongly implicit argument within them. The moral of 'Little Red Riding Hood' can be that Red Riding Hood should not have disobeyed her mother in talking to the wolf, though her mistake is rectified by the timely entrance of the woodcutter. A child actively construing that story and matching its metaphoric reality with real life could not escape its implicit argument/moral. The narrative structure which allows the argument/moral to be discovered by the reader, rather than its being more obviously exposed by argument, is possibly more acceptable at a young age. Readers can discover the meanings themselves and those meanings may vary according to psychic needs. Some versions of fairy tales endorse this principle. The point is that some narratives embody within their structure subtle arguments which are perceptible even to young readers. Of necessity, because teachers and researchers need to agree upon terms of reference in order to discuss children's language development, models or paradigms become a currency in such discussions.

A preoccupation with kinds, types, forms, genres – whatever we call them – is a concern of a teacher but not of a writer. Writers are concerned with creating meanings in language. If a certain form helps to shape that meaning, it will be incorporated into the complex process of writing. Awareness of different forms adds to the internalized repertoire of language use upon which the writer draws for the creative symbolic act of writing. But knowledge of forms is not, in itself, a sufficient resource for development as a writer. The ability to integrate aspects of experience in writing by drawing upon the vast resources of the human mind (thoughts, feelings, conscious and unconscious images, memories, wishes, and so on) is an important characteristic of a maturing writer. Perhaps I should now exemplify my own argument with a story.

The argument is that writers often use an interplay of forms to achieve their purposes, providing simultaneously an interesting texture to their writing through the contrast effect of that interplay. In oral speech the evangelical preacher comes to mind. He/she knows how to present an impassioned argument supported by stories drawn from various sources. In a sense that is what I am doing here: arguing for a closer perception of the value of an interplay of discourse forms in children's writing. The evidence to support this is drawn from an analysis of children's written texts and from the story of a piece of research. Argument alone can be overly didactic; the narrative effects will, hopefully, enrich the discourse.

Let me recount parts of a longitudinal research study I undertook for four years with thirty-five selected students in (school) Years 6–9 inclusive. Essentially the study involved my working with groups each of about sixteen students in two Sydney metropolitan schools. I undertook a particular writing intervention programme with the groups, starting in Year 6 and following through with them to the end of Year 9.

The main purpose was to see whether or not the writing development of the experimental group was significantly greater than that of the control groups. After initial difficulties with holistic marking where markers failed to perceive significant development in writing for either the control or the experimental groups, four criteria guidelines were devised: *audience, creativity, thinking* and *language*.

When markers re-marked the scripts for each of the four criteria, and their results were analysed, some development could be discerned over the four-year period, with a significant improvement in the *thinking* category for the experimental group.

Of relevance to this chapter was the difficulty markers experienced in perceiving developmental trends in students' writing until some framework was provided which guided their marking and put in perspective the influence of the set topic. What I am suggesting is the value of categories, or genres, or modes in establishing sets for readers' or markers' purposes. But in the classroom such category systems need to be used subtly and appropriately.

The test results arose from the annual writing tasks set for the experimental and control groups. In Year 6 the following topic was set:

> Imagine you have met a friendly visitor from outer space. The visitor came to your school to find out why children write. Could you write him a letter telling him what is easy or hard about writing tasks, why you do them and what makes them enjoyable? Try to help him as much as you can by telling him your ideas and feelings about writing.

Obviously I designed the topic so that the writers could perceive themselves as writing in the role of experts to the space visitor who is ignorant of the purposes for writing in school. Arguably, had I simply asked the writers to list the reasons why we write in school, or to argue why writing should be part of school life, I would not have received as many committed, engaging and well-differentiated points of view about the purpose of writing as I did. That is, the invitation to *tell* about an aspect of school life was taken up by some students as an invitation to go beyond telling to expressing some embryonic point of view about writing, with an implicit evaluation of its worth. That is, those students who perceive a 'prompt' (topic) as an invitation to exploration, rather than as merely an imperative to report, do play the variables of narrative and argument. They recognize, or at least demonstrate to an alert reader, that the full effectiveness of narrative sometimes depends on the readers' ability to read between the lines, while argument allows the writer's point of view to be highlighted and explicated.

Parallel with this ability to exploit the potential of the interplay between narrative and argument is some awareness of the need to be implicit or explicit according to context and purpose. How writers learn when to be explicit and when to be implicit is another story. Suffice to say here that an interplay between kinds of written discourse shows at least the writer's awareness of the ends served by movements across more or less explicit or implicit modes. That is, these writers perceive and exploit a function in interrelating kinds of writing. They can choose, often unconsciously, those features or aspects of written genres which match their discourse intentions.

The topic for Year 9 in the research project was the following:

> Imagine you are living in a futuristic age where it is possible to buy a plan for your future life from a 'life-plan agent'. [The life-plan agent is rather like a travel agent

who consults with you about what you want and helps you put together the best plan.] You like the idea of being able to choose your future life and decide you will go to the life-plan agent. Before you do so you write to a close friend discussing with him/her what you think you would like that plan to be.

Your plans could include living in other countries or in space, having an interesting career, becoming famous, making a fortune, working to improve conditions on earth, having great adventures or whatever your imagination dreams of.

As you are living in a futuristic age you can be as practical and as imaginative as you like. The friend you are writing to could have some part in your future life or could just be someone to share your ideas with now. (Please sign the letter with your own name.)

The intention behind the formulation of this topic was to invite writers to think in speculative, imaginative ways.

For contrast purposes I will confine my examples of students' writing to samples from the end of Year 6 and the end of Year 9 to examine how the ability to interplay narrative and argument influences the writers' effectiveness.

Consider Tina's Year 6 and Year 9 letters:

Dear Zondoim,
I enjoy writing very much. No, writing tasks are not difficult. My favourite writing tasks are creative writing and poetry. I sometimes would rather write in a lesson than have an oral lesson. What people try to do in creative writing is to thrill the reader and to keep them in suspense until the creative writing or book is finished. People read and write usually for enjoyment. In poetry there are two different kinds of verse: blank verse and rhyming verse. Blank verse is very blank e.g. 'worry not my dear, for I shall maketh you a home with thine hands'.

Rhyming verse rhymes e.g. 'worry not my dear, for Tina the great is here.'

When a person is writing facts about something, they usually don't think of what they're writing. But when a person tries to put facts into their own words, they usually read the sentence and then put it into their own words and that way they learn something about what they're writing.
Love,
Tina.

Dear Blank,
I went into the life-plan agent yesterday to check out what they were offering. It's pretty impressive. I can plan my life on any planet, or in any country that I want, doing what I want. I've got to choose between four of them:

I can either go to Ireland and be a vet there. I hear that they're got some of the nicest natural landscapes, so they'll have animals. And, seeing how I can speak all one hundred and thirty two animal languages, it wouldn't be too hard doing that.

Or, I could go to France and join in the French resistance for the war they're having with Spain. But that would be dangerous, as I can always get killed there.

Or, I could go to the middle-east and be a doctor in Israel. That would be interesting and the climate is a lot like it is here.

Or, I could be a jet-setting socialite, except that the world is full of them ever since that great discovery of the new metal. No one wants to work any more seeing how they can always let this metal run their houses. Maybe I'll be the guy who actually discovered it, you see, I can go back or forward in time. It would be a bit of a nuisance though, if people popped in and out of everyday life – Hi Frank, oh, bye Frank – I mean the world would be full of people popping back and forward in time.

The ideal place, I think, would be like a place I read about in the archives. It was by this great scholar called Dr Zeus wrote all these books for kids. Anyway, this book was called – 'oh, the thinks you can think'. The pictures are the best. I'd love to zap myself there, except I'd be one of them, and life would be interesting instead of dull.

Another time I'd like to be in would be during the eighteenth century in France, with all the aristocrats leading exciting lives, going to balls and parties.

In the first of these, Tina is clearly focusing on argument – generalizing about writing from her own experience and providing supporting evidence for her point of view. (Her final paragraph should give heart to experience-centred writing teachers!) Three years later in her second letter we can witness a skilful interplay of argument and fantasy-narrative. The ability to switch across past, present and future time is impressive. The topic itself was deliberately structured to invite students to speculate on a future life and to share that speculation with a friend prior to the visit to the life-plan agent. Quite complex shifts in time, audience, and imagination were built into the topic. Tina took up many of the implicit and explicit options suggested by the topic and wove her own fantasy-argument. Whether we call her letter an argument or a fantasy is not as important as recognizing the cognitive, linguistic and imaginative resources she has called upon to write her letter. She knows she can leave largely implicit the reference to the discovery of the new metal; after all she is writing to a friend who shares part of her context, even though Tina also knows that the letter finally finishes up with the researcher. We can recognize some of the ideas she has internalized from history and from her reading of fantasies and imaginative stories. But the most lasting impression is of a writer centred in the experience of dynamically reconstructing memories and ideas in a creative, engaging way. The interplay between argument and narrative creates contrast and texture in the writing and we are left in no doubt about the writer's authentic exploration of future life possibilities. Arguably, the most effective writing, in whatever form, gives us an insight into the writer's mind and writing processes which transcends debates about the relative merits of rhetorical forms.

For contrast, let us consider the letters of another writer, John. Here is his Year 6 letter:

Dear Tocarty,
How are you, in school we write all the time so we can learn. Do you write? Do you go to school? You look so funny, why do you have antennaes on your head, are you a human? Can you write? In school you find reading very hard and writing very easy. All you got to do is learn the alphabet and then you learn how to write words. I like doing spelling because you learn millions and millions of new words and you have games and you learn to read.

Tocarty, I'll teach you how to write, it will be fun. Please come again to our school.

Yours Sincerely,

John's capacity to argue is limited to fairly concrete statements of fact – 'learn the alphabet . . . to write words' – and the recording of some feelings about writing. None the less, there is an engaging quality in the writing, in the rhetorical questions, and in the entreaty to Tocarty to 'come again to our school' which creates yet again an impression of a writer actively creating his letter to an imaginary spaceman.

Let us now consider John's Year 9 letter:

David,

I went to a life plan agent and they planned my life and you don't even have to work. The agent said you can go on the dole all life and still do all the pleasures you would like to do. I thought you would be interested in this, because all you do is like to surf.

So, he's got an old hut for us because we don't need a good house because it will cost too much to run, and it's right on a beach. He said besides surfing you can shape surf boards for the locals who live there and make a bit of money. For the food and money because it cost money for food we will grow our own.

For electricity we don't need because we will use a lot of candles and for warmth a big fire because we have a chimney. If we run out of money we will go in to surfing competitions to win money. By the way if we lived on the beach and go surfing every day we will be the best. Then we can go on to bigger things like getting sponsored and getting our boards free and wetsuits and go to other countries to compete in surfing events and there's big money in that.

Then if we win we will be rich and the best surfers in the world. Then we go on to more bigger things like going to other worlds to compete with their best surfers. So, if you want to do this life plan, write me back to say what you have decided so we will be going places.

It is easy to see that this invitation to fantasy caught John's imagination. It is also easy to see differences between his control of time and space dimensions in writing and Tina's. In Tina's Year 9 letter we can visualize Tina playing out possibilities with an awareness of the differences between fantasy and reality. In John's letter there is a sense of nearly complete immersion in the fantasy with a loss of any critical or self-scrutinizing faculty. His form of arguing is to claim omnipotence – 'you can go on the dole all life' and 'If we run out of money we will go in to surfing competitions to win money'. He fails to see that a lot of candles may not substitute for electricity. However, while we can argue that John interplays argument and fantasy-narrative in his letter, and it is possible to sense his real engagement in the writing experience, why would we regard Tina's writing as more mature than John's (as did a number of markers)? Maturity as a writer clearly involves more than an ability to use different forms of writing, or even an interplay of those forms.

I would suggest that writing maturity is an ability in Tina's case to incorporate both argument and narrative in her writing, to differentiate between fantasy and reality, to explore time and space dimensions imaginatively, and to see herself as part of an interactive social world to which she can give, and from which she can take. These abilities take us then into the realm of the cognitive ability to decentre as an individual and to differentiate experience.

Development as a writer does depend on more than the ability to use effectively various language forms: there is also the need to think in increasingly more complex and differentiated ways and both to analyse and to negotiate experience. Certain writing experiences can help develop language and thinking but in many schools insufficient time is given to the task. In addition, schools are only part of the educating process. In real life John's main preoccupation was surfing, and Tina's was books and learning. From the profoundly complex experience of working with both students for the four years of the research study (Tina developed significantly better as a writer than her peers in the control group; John did not), I am more aware of the complexity of issues influencing writing development than I was before I started. I am also less confident than ever that simple answers, like more teaching of genres or forms, will help. Would an understanding of discourse forms help John become a better writer? Tina was interested in different forms because writing was of long-term personal significance to her. Even in Year 6 she had a more complex view of writing and of her own metacognitive processes than John had in Year 9 (but neither she nor I would care about the shape of surfboards!).

Having moved from arguing for an awareness of interplay between narrative and argument in children's writing, I am now arguing that even that awareness is insufficient. There will always be writers who fail to develop competence with forms and writers who go beyond that competence. It is what goes beyond or below the forms which can be both revealing and baffling. Consider the personality behind these two letters:

Dear Mr friendly visitor from outer space,
I've been told to write you a letter, so here I am. There is one thing I despise about writing, thinking up ideas. If I'm in the mood I'm fine but if I'm not, lets not talk about that. Trying to be different but original is very difficult. I'm quite good at descriptive words but the theme never seems right. I suppose I'll have to admit if I'm in the mood I just take off like a rocket and write about a three page story, but if I'm not . . .
   One thing I enjoy about writing is when it's a good topic and I can be creative. Millions of ideas flash into my head and I sit for hours. Might I add an awful lot of that time is taken up by writing new stories and throwing out the rest.
   Like I said I've been told to write. My teacher tells me everything I've got to write. The only thing she doesn't tell me is the story, and thats left all for me. If I could make up everything I'm sure I'd write a better, more interesting, story.
   I hope I've been helpful to you in your research,
Yours Sincerely,

Dear Bill,

I'm well, I hope you are too. I've just been to visit the life-plan agent and everything's set. I've an appointment with him in 1 month and he's given me all this wonderful time to plan the rest of my life. Unfortunately, I've already planned to the last detail, all the way down to the names of the poodles so I'll just sit and twiddle my thumbs for the rest of the month. There's one little tiny weeny problem, which is: we have to be married sometime in the last month. Now I appreciate that I leave everything up to you, women always do, so I've taken the liberty to ask you to marry me. 'Will you marry me'. I know you'll say yes, so we'll organise the details in a week. We have to wait a week because I'm about to enter a deep sleep for 7 days. It's part of my beauty plan. Oh dear! Gorilla 1,008 is getting worked up because I'm due at the beauty salon in 20 minutes. He's my new robot and although efficient he's very tiresome at times. How you say 'tres bien mais ne pas tres bien'. That's French for very good but not very good, in case you're not educated.

Let me tell you about our life ahead. It's hassle free with no strings attached. We live a life of primitives. No more multi-million dollar parties, socials, cards, affairs with best-friends husbands, no more. We're being transformed to a cave in another time galaxy. There's an abundant supply of food, no doors out, no doors in. It'll be just like our own pumpkin. We'll just stay in a cave and make babies all day.

No more time to talk, bell's gone, ring you later sweety,

Much love.

I defy anyone to argue that a knowledge of genres or forms made a significant contribution to that piece of writing. And I defy anyone to analyse it in a way which enriches the experience of reading it.

Clearly, children's language development is dependent upon exposure to a rich and varied range of language functions and models. Small children are capable of arguing in a rudimentary way (especially when their wishes are thwarted) and it is true that report, narrating and fantasizing are their most common written forms until secondary school. Possibly pupils can argue and narrate equally well or badly depending on their perception of the audience, purpose and intrinsic worth of the task. If they need to communicate to achieve an end (either an object or to 'save face') argument is chosen; if they need implicitly to integrate experiences then narrative fulfils that function. There may be greater dependency in an argument on the reader's concurrence with a point of view or personal perception, while in narrative the construction of an experience, and possibly an exploration of it, may be an end in itself.

Both narrative and argument are valid and necessary in the development of writing and thinking maturity because both allow the process of differentiation to occur and, in turn, demonstrate that process. By arguing or narrating we can articulate a particular perception of the experience we are symbolizing. That articulation may influence only our own differentiation, or it may influence others as well.

To argue that either narrative or argument is more powerful is to deny the necessary integrity of the world of discourse. To return to my opening point, the differentiation of, say, certain forms of discourse into narrative and argument is a convenient research tool. It allows us to simplify and to generalize discourse so that we can share common understandings with colleagues. Paradoxically, that attempt to categorize written discourse can only take us so far. Even cursory analysis of written texts reveals their much greater complexity and richness than models or categories or paradigms can suggest. None the less, it would be worth knowing at what point, if any, it is crucial for writers to be able to recognize different forms.

Certainly an interplay between kinds of discourse can demonstrate the writer's recognition (probably unconscious) that the range of discourse types enhances our capacity to perceive the world as infinitely rich and variable and the structures of language as potentially available to demonstrate that richness. How conscious that recognition needs to become is arguable.

My own argument here has depended upon the elaboration of a point of view with selected examples from children's writing. It is my hope that the most memorable parts of this essay will be those examples. It is my belief that close encounters with children's language demonstrate that the need teachers/ researchers may have for category systems is subsidiary. The unequivocally more powerful need we have is to engage with the individual minds behind the text.

# 7 Contexts for developing argument

## AVIVA FREEDMAN AND IAN PRINGLE

In Canada, when students write at school, they write primarily in two modes. There are occasional forays into poetry or reflective personal essays, and recently some attempts at expressive writing in journals, but the dominant emphasis is on writing narrative, and what we call 'argument'. (The latter term may need further definition, and we shall return to it. Suffice it to say for the moment that writing argument is not the same as being argumentative in writing.)

Over the past few years, we have been conducting research on several fronts, aimed at understanding development in typical school-sponsored writing. One question arises from the clear differences in student performance and development in the two modes of narrative and argument. A few years ago, in an article entitled 'Why Students Can't Write Arguments' (Freedman and Pringle 1984), we explored these differences and discussed their possible causes. Since then, further research has led us to refine these earlier notions as well as to develop our thinking in new directions. Our interest continues to be not so much in differences between the two forms of writing but rather in what these differences reveal about how students learn to write in general and how those about them facilitate this learning.

## The research

The following discussion grows primarily out of a series of studies examining student writing in Ontario. We have now conducted four such studies (Freedman and Pringle 1979; 1980; 1984; Pringle and Freedman 1985), three of which involved the entire population of one or more school boards in specific grades and ability levels. (The numbers of students involved is thus in the tens of thousands.) The grades selected have always been some or all of grade 5; grade 8 (the last year in our elementary system); and grade 12 (the last year in the secondary system for students who are not university-bound). At the grade 12 level, we have drawn separate samples from 12A or 'advanced' students, who are university-bound, and the 12G or 'general' students.

In each study, we elicited writing from all students in the relevant grades and levels within the participating school boards. The nature of the assignment was intended to reflect typical curricular goals, both in what was assigned and in how the writing was elicited. Thus in the largest study (Pringle and Freedman 1985), half the students were asked to write arguments, and half narratives. (Of those writing narratives, half wrote true stories and half wrote invented ones.)

In all the studies the classroom teachers themselves elicited the writing in a prescribed format which allowed for unconstrained generation of ideas in or out of class as well as multiple-draft composing. Specifically, students were given the writing topic several days in advance. Then, one day was devoted to developing a first draft, and a second to revising that draft. While far from ideal, such a structure allowed for a process considerably closer to a normal composing process than the typical one-shot writing assignment of most large-scale studies, to say nothing of most tests and examinations.

The wording of the assignment in each case specified the mode but left the topic open. The prompt for the argument was worded as follows:

> There are probably things happening in the world around you – at school, among your friends, at home, in the country, in the world – that you think ought to be changed. Select one and write a composition (or an essay, or an article, or letter) to convince someone else (preferably someone who has the power to make changes) that what you object to is really bad and ought to be changed.

The narrative prompts were equally open, involving elaborations of each of the following: for the true or personal narrative, 'write a short story about something that happened to you personally or to someone you know'; for the invented narrative, 'write a short story about some imaginary event'. In each case, the goal was to see what students could do by themselves given open topics and some allowance for different composing rhythms and styles – given, in short, what Nancy Martin (1986) has described as 'scope for intention'.

## The analyses

The scripts which we obtained as a result of these assignments were examined using a range of analytic instruments, each probing a different dimension of the writing. The analyses revealed some patterns of development to be common to both the narratives and arguments: affective growth along the lines suggested by Wilkinson *et al.* (1980); increases in the degree of elaboration and specification; increased command of the linguistic resources of the language. Development in the degree of realization of the conventional structure for the genre was also common to both – with the following important difference. Whereas the student writers uniformly displayed a mastery of at least the basic elements of story structure by the end of elementary school, for the arguments there was no such uniform control – even by the end of secondary school. In other words, for both arguments and narratives, there was development towards greater control over the conventional form; this was achieved quite early for the narratives, whereas for the arguments there was a considerable time-lag. The nature and degree of the control, as well as possible reasons for the time-lag, are considered below.

## Story structure

In order to define student success in creating stories that satisfy the requirements for a narrative in our culture, we developed a simple instrument for describing story structure, basing it on the rich literature on the subject in discourse and literary analysis. (For a more detailed discussion, see Freedman 1987.) In simple terms, to qualify as a story in our scheme a piece of writing would have to include some information about the setting as well as at least one complete episode, a complete episode being one in which a protagonist responds to an initiating event, primarily through goal-orientated behaviour.

When the students' writing was examined according to these criteria, clear patterns emerged. First, as children get older there is overall development towards greater realization of the basic form, with differences by type of story. For invented stories, by grade 8 almost all the narratives embody the conventional structure; for the true stories, however, there is a time-lag so that it is only by grade 12 (both for advanced and general levels) that the basic structure is realized for all stories. Moreover, the control of story structure, especially among invented stories, is such that older student writers often play with the form – deliberately reversing and withholding conventional patterns to make their point. For example, in one grade 12 story, the writer initially upsets the readers' expectations of goal-orientated behaviour in order to probe the assumptions behind such expectations. These are instances of 'post-conventional' discourse, in which the mastery of conventional forms and structures is so complete that the writer is able to stand above, as it were, to comment on and play with the forms themselves.

## Structure of the arguments

In the North American tradition of composition teaching, 'argument' holds a central place. As noted above, writing argument is not the same as being argumentative in writing. Rather, argument refers to a mode which is first defined and exemplified in classical rhetoric and whose characteristics have been repeatedly discussed since then, not only in the North American rhetorical tradition, but also in the Scottish tradition which is, in part, its source. Conventional formulations see written arguments as organized around a clear thesis (either implicit, or more commonly explicit) which is substantiated logically and through illustration in the body of the piece. The nature of the logic can be defined more precisely, as can many of the stylistic and organizational features. In our study, however, we developed as an instrument for the initial description of the data only a minimal set of criteria for argumentative structure. To satisfy our norms, a written argument needed only a clear thesis (either explicit or implicit from the beginning) and a substantiating set of logically developed points and/or illustrations proving the thesis and forming the body of the essay.

These criteria were satisfied by fewer than 30 per cent of the grade 5 essays, about 40 per cent of the grade 8 essays, fewer than 50 per cent of the 12G pieces, and 65 per cent of the 12A pieces. In other words, while there was a steady progression upwards, even the 12A students had not achieved the kind of mastery of argument achieved by the grade 8 students in their writing of invented stories. If one can characterize the writing of stories in the upper grades as that of master craftsmen, in their writing of arguments, the students revealed themselves to be apprentices or journeymen.

## Why?

In 'Why Students Can't Write Arguments' (Freedman and Pringle 1984), we reported on data which showed similar tendencies and advanced the following set of possible explanations for the differences between student control of conventional structures in stories and arguments. First, from their earliest years, children are exposed to written narratives: stories are read to them and the first books they themselves read are typically stories. They do not read arguments, nor are arguments read to them. Second, oral narratives offer a model for written narratives in a way that is not true of arguments. The pattern of oral argumentation is that of a tennis match where each shot is parried by one's partner, with the further complication that each shot may change the direction of the argument so that the end may be played on very different territory. There is no requirement (and little likelihood) of internal logical consistency or patterning. Thus, in learning to write arguments, the novice writer must acquire another skill – the ability to discover and/or create a rigorously logical structure which will unify and order the individual points generated. A further explanation of the difference in performance, then, lies in the fact that structuring in arguments requires an abstracting ability analogous to that which Vygotsky (1978) describes in his discussion of concept formation.

Without ascribing any less explanatory power to these interpretations, we would like to offer a new perspective. New data, as well as new ways of analysing the data, have allowed us to consider the problem afresh.

## Further distinctions

In order to understand differences in student performance in narrative and argument, we decided to look more carefully at those papers that were not conventional arguments. Two patterns were apparent. First, there were large numbers of papers which seemed exploratory in character (though the proportion of these decreased as the students' age increased); second, as the age of the students increased, there was an increased proportion of papers which were conative (to use a term from Britton *et al.* 1975) or persuasive, rather than (in our technical sense) argumentative.

## Writing to explore

Most of the writing at the grade 5 level, and almost one-third at the grade 12 level, could be described as exploratory in character – what Dixon and Stratta (1982a) characterize as 'ruminative' writing. Such writing aims to capture the immediate responses of the writer to the topic or follows the writer's attempt to come to terms with the notions selected. Here is a typical example at grade 12A level:

> There are many institutions in the country today that require change, not the least is the school system. Now being a student, I must confess a certain bias, however it is the student who is probably the most qualified to suggest change, seeing how he is the one with firsthand experience.
>
> The concept of school is sound. Any intelligent person realizes the importance of learning and its benefit to both the individual and society. However being cooped up in a succession of frighteningly stark rooms for upwards of seven hours a day hardly seems to fit the bill. The purpose of education is not only to educate, but to hopefully inspire, challenge, and enrich the individual. The view from here as I listen to the daily moans and groans of fellow students indicates all too graphically that the school system at present is not fulfilling these objectives . . .
>
> On reading this essay over, I'm struck by the cynicism of it. Given some thought, many of these frustrations and complaints are largely seasonal. Spring fever and the approaching summer holidays are too insistent to ignore. Yes, the school system needs improving, but changes and progress in education will only occur as a result of farsighted and progressive administrators in conjunction with pressure from the students. Hopefully the school system of ten years hence will be unrecognizable with that of today, and with any luck at all, it will be for the better.

The writer is here exploring the subject matter: on the basis of expressing his attitude in its most extreme form, he discovers the limitations of that position, and ends on a more balanced note. (This is not an uncharacteristic pattern.) The writing itself has forced or allowed for a new understanding: the draft is a discovery draft.

This kind of writing can be viewed in one of two ways: it may represent an early draft – a first stage in the writing of a particular piece. On the other hand, it may be the kind of writing that occurs when a student has not yet reached the stage, with respect to the material covered, when she or he can stand above it sufficiently to find an overarching generalization – a thesis to unify the material. In other words, this writing may either represent a stage in the writing of specific pieces or a cognitive developmental stage. Such writing may indicate that students do not know how to revise their pieces, how to move through the composing process towards the presentation of a final draft. Alternatively, the predominance of such writing may indicate writers who have not yet reached an appropriate cognitive level to handle their material.

Evidence from analyses performed on the nature of the revisions to first drafts indicated that many students did not, in fact, revise, in the sense of re-see, their early drafts. The kind of restructuring that is a normal stage in the composing process of many experienced writers did not take place. It is precisely this kind of restructuring that might have transformed the scripts from exploratory or expressive writing to argumentation in the conventional sense.

The question that arises is why such restructuring did not occur, given that there was opportunity for revising. Several reasons suggest themselves. First, the students may simply have lacked the strategies for effective revising. (Other evidence suggests that this is the case.) Alternatively or additionally, the students may have lacked the internalized model for argument which could function as a guide to revision. And finally, even if they had both the ability to revise and the appropriate internalized model, they might not have been able, at this stage of their development, to make the abstractive leap upwards required to structure their arguments appropriately.

The latter point bears some elaboration. As we suggested earlier, shaping an argument implies an abstractive act similar to that described by Vygotsky (1962) in his discussion of concept-formation. What must be stressed is that this ability to form concepts is not something that is acquired once and for all. As the data from which one must abstract change, so do the nature and potential difficulty of the task of abstracting.

Consider the following. One of our most cogently expressed and effectively organized pieces of argumentation was produced by a grade 8 student, arguing for a change in the number of games in the quarter-round hockey finals from five to seven. Compare the nature of the data as well as the level of abstracting required in such a task to that entailed on the grade 12A essay discussing the nature of the school system. Clearly, the complexity of the task undertaken by each writer was a crucial factor in his performance.

Exploratory writing may be an inevitable consequence of writers wrestling with notions just beyond their easy grasp. As long as students define their tasks in ways that involve their stretching upwards along the abstractive continuum, one consequence may be a failure in the realization of the conventional structure for arguments. If this is so, such a failure is a small price to pay for the growth implied.

## Distracting models

As we have noted, while there was a decrease in the percentage of exploratory pieces as students matured, there was an increase in the proportion of scripts whose function was more akin to what Britton *et al.* (1975) define as conative or persuasive. In a classification of discourse that he rightly describes as parallel to that of Britton *et al.* (1975), Kinneavy (1980) distinguishes persuasive writing from writing to prove a thesis (what we call argument), by pointing to the former's hortatory tone (the reader is often specifically evoked and involved), as well as its emotion-laden language and style. Exclamations are frequent, as are value-laden terms and images that tug at one's heartstrings or arouse one's anger. There is considerable appeal through what Aristotle calls the 'pathetic' argument – based on our emotions. There is limited appeal to reason, although an appearance of factuality and evidence is sometimes sought. (Advertising and political speeches are classic examples of the category.)

In contrast, in a piece designed to prove a thesis both the author and the audience are, at least superficially, invisible. The focus is on the subject matter and the appeal is through carefully articulated and developed logical argumentation. Value-laden words – indeed strongly colourful language in general – are avoided, while the case is made entirely on logical and factual grounds in as impersonal and objective a tone as possible (Kinneavy 1971).

By categorizing the essays according to this distinction we discovered an increasing number of persuasive pieces by age and grade level, so that by grade 12 over 20 per cent of the essays were of this kind. The following example is typical.

> Have you ever noticed, while eating lunch at school, at a restaurant or even in your own home how much food is being thrown out or given to the family pet. This is not necessary! This food can be kept for the next day or even put into other foods that you eat daily. People should realize that food is not going to go down in price, it is only going to rise. Learn to conserve food as well as electricity. Cook less food, and realize how much this food is costing you. Remember the children in the foreign countries who are starving and withering away to die. Think before you throw away that food, that you could be saving a life instead of killing one.

This student has captured the hortatory tone, the appeal to emotions, the condescension and superficiality of advertising. It is this mode of discourse, rather than argument, which has functioned as a model. Given the influence of TV advertisements and other forms of public propaganda, and given the form of much homiletic material directed towards students (on drugs, alcohol, cigarettes, etc.), it is hardly surprising that an increasing number of pieces are shaped in this way. Part of what teachers need to do to help their students is to combat the effect of such distracting models of discourse.

## Models

While inappropriate models of persuasive discourse abound, students are rarely exposed to appropriate models of argumentation. We suggested earlier that young children are not exposed to written arguments as they are to written stories. For many students that situation does not change much over the course of their school years. Typical reading over these years consists primarily of fiction and, for school, textbooks which are informative rather than argumentative (to use Kinneavy's distinction) in aim and structure. Some students may read newspaper editorials and argumentative pieces in sports or fashion magazines, but such writing is not likely to form a significant part of student reading over those years.

In fact, given the poverty of their exposure, it is surprising that students acquire the structure of argumentation at all. That they do so is clearly a result of something other than modelling. How, then, do they do so? An attempt to understand how students succeed when they do succeed provided another perspective on why many failed.

### School concepts

An important clue was provided by those papers which were written on what are clearly school-related or school-taught topics. Pollution, for example, figured largely, and more specifically acid rain, as well as nuclear energy, and nutrition and health. Essays on such subjects were written at all four grades and levels, and almost always their structure satisfied our minimal requirements for argument. More than this, in comparison to the other essays, these papers were remarkably cogent, highly substantiated, and confidently argued.

In order to explain this phenomenon, we drew on Vygotsky's (1962) distinction between scientific and spontaneous or everyday concepts. Scientific concepts he defined as those which are introduced to the child through explicit instruction, especially in the context of school subjects. Everyday concepts are those which arise naturally through experience. Vygotsky shows that scientific concepts are presented within hierarchical systems of interrelationships in a way not true of spontaneous or everyday concepts. This explains why it is easier to write in a structured, organized way about scientific or school concepts. Because such concepts have been presented in the context of carefully articulated systems of ideas, organizing structures for the writing are more readily accessible – not because such structures are handed over ready-made but because the scientific or content-area teaching both models and elicits the kinds of thinking necessary in order to find such organizing structures.

Most of the student arguments were not so orchestrated, focusing as they did on spontaneous or everyday notions, rather than scientific or school-related concepts. Typical topics grew out of personal experience or general issues of communal concern (war, the economy, values, etc.). Normally such issues are not dealt with in any formal systematic fashion in the students' experience; they tend to be discussed casually, without the structured and orderly treatment inherent in school instruction.

This is not to denigrate the kind of loose unstructured talk around personal or general topics that takes place in small-group discussions in and out of school. However, whatever the other values of this talk – and they are many – it does not elicit from the participants the kind of thinking coincident with, or leading towards, the patterning of argumentative essays. (Indeed, this very fact may point to the particular power of talk, which allows for and contributes to a kind of understanding that is different from, although often drawn on by, the kind of understanding that is prized in academic discourse.) For this reason, essays on personal or general topics are inherently more difficult to structure than those focusing on scientific or school-related concepts.

## Pedagogic scaffolding

To put it another way, students who wrote about school-related concepts were provided with a kind of pedagogic framework not given to those writing about personal experiences or general public issues. The nature of this framework is worth exploring in some detail because of what may be revealed about the way in which students learn to write arguments specifically and about how they acquire forms in general.

One of the co-authors of this piece (Freedman) has been involved in an observational study investigating how students go about acquiring the new kinds of writing expected of them at university. Specifically, students were observed in an introductory undergraduate course in Law as they learned to produce the kind of writing that was clearly distinct from all the other writing (academic, personal, and business) which they had produced or were producing, and different as well from any models to which they were exposed in their reading. Astonishingly, every student observed realized this new and idiosyncratic form in their writing; furthermore, this extraordinary feat was accomplished not through explicit teaching or exposure to models – but through a complex, intricate and largely tacit collaboration between instructors and students.

The nature of this collaboration is instructive. The term 'collaboration' is not intended in the narrow sense of conscious and focused interaction over writing. In fact, there was no interaction with students over work-in-progress; nor was there any careful, consciously contrived staging of subtasks within the larger task. The collaboration was more subtle, less deliberate, and less obvious to the participants.

The writing of the assignments was an intricate, extended collaborative performance, in which each of the players took an active role. The whole interaction began well before the first assignment was set. Through his lectures, the professor dramatized the kinds of topic appropriate for discussions in Law – as well as the kinds of argument that may legitimately be brought to bear according to the conventions of the discipline. (For example, in the context of legal analysis, no attention is paid to the personal or emotional consequences of losing the suit – either for the client or the lawyer.) Similarly, in their discussions both the professor and the teaching assistant illustrated the kinds of evidence and the kinds of reasoning valued by the discipline. Then, by setting the assignment, the instructor defined the data and posed the kind of question that could elicit from the students the kinds of thinking appropriate to thinking about Law.

In all these ways, the writing of the Law students was shaped by the professor. He set up a pedagogic framework in which students could enact through their writing the kinds of thinking appropriate to the discipline; in doing so, they commonly and communally created a form that was the objective correlate of such thinking.

Vygotsky (1978) argues that, from infancy on, children learn and develop cognitively through social interaction with adults. More precisely, through collaborative performance of specific tasks with adults, children learn to perform the tasks by themselves. The Law class we observed provided a more sophisticated version of precisely such collaborative performance.

If we turn now to a typical composition classroom, at least in North America, a very different scenario can be observed. In comparison to what transpired in the Law class, composition assignments are elicited in a relative vacuum. There may be some attempt to orchestrate a few minutes of general discussion, or perhaps some diffuse communal brainstorming of ideas; however, there is nothing like the extended shaping and contextualizing of basic notions, the interactive dramatizing of lines of reasoning and grounds for arguing which precede the writing of discipline-specific arguments. Should we wonder that, in comparison to the discipline-specific pieces, the typical composition-class arguments seem to lack centre, direction, focus and structure?

## Transferring learning

As an interesting side-note, the preceding discussion may explain not only how students acquire form in discipline-specific arguments, but also how their more general and personal pieces come to embody the conventional structure for arguments. As our data revealed, even among the more general and personal typical composition pieces, there was a development over the years, from grades 5 to 8 to 12G to 12A, towards greater realization of the conventional form. Since this development cannot be explained by significantly increased exposure to appropriate models (it is not clear that there was such an increase in exposure), then one must look elsewhere for an explanation.

Vygotsky's discussion of the interaction between instruction and development provides just such an explanation. Vygotsky (1962, p. 93) argues that 'the rudiments of systemization first enter the child's mind by way of his contact with scientific concepts and *are then transferred to everyday concepts*' (emphasis added). In other words, as a result of their exposure to scientific concepts, children become progressively more able to systematize their everyday concepts. In the context of writing, this suggests that, as a result of writing arguments about scientific concepts, as a result of writing arguments about school-related subjects, students acquire the ability to write pieces that incorporate the norms for argument in their compositions about personal experience and general public issues.

All this implies a reversal of the conventional assumptions about learning to write, at least in North America. Typically, responsibility for the teaching of writing is laid at the door of the English specialist, the belief being that strategies and skills acquired in the composition class will transfer to content-area writing. We must entertain the possibility that at least some of the transference is in the other direction; that less responsibility need be placed at the door of the English specialist; and that more respect is due to the disciplinary teachers of writing.

## Conclusion

To sum up, three kinds of evidence in our data proved suggestive. First, a significant proportion of responses to the argumentative assignments were, in fact, exploratory or expressive in nature. Second, an increasing percentage of scripts were persuasive, rather than argumentative. And third, those pieces which focused on scientific or school-related topics were structured more appropriately than those dealing with personal experience or subjects of a general public nature.

These different kinds of evidence point to the following possible explanations for the relative lack of mastery of conventional argumentative structure in student writing:

1 The high proportion of exploratory pieces pointed in one of two directions, or in a combination of the two. First, it may be that many students simply have not been taught the revising strategies necessary for restructuring their initial exploratory drafts; the failure may be one of craftsmanship. Alternatively or additionally, students may be cognitively unable to rise sufficiently above the notions presented in their pieces to find or create the unifying pattern necessary for argumentative structure. The failure, then, may signal writers not yet in control of the concepts – a phenomenon that is likely to recur as long as writers continue to reach upwards.

2 Students may err, in their writing of arguments, because of their exposure to inappropriate models. A significant number of pieces were influenced by the model of persuasive discourse so predominant in our culture through advertising and political propaganda. Furthermore, against this distracting and inappropriate model, there is no sufficiently strong counterbalancing exposure to appropriate models. Students do not, on the whole, read much argumentative discourse even at the grade 12 level.

3 The kind of pedagogic scaffolding offered in content-area classes is not erected in many composition classes. The writing of arguments in the composition class is not facilitated and shaped as in the content-areas.

All this may mean that we must rethink what our students read, what our students are expected to write, and especially how we facilitate their writing and learning. Some of the issues raised are amenable to direct action on the part of the writing teacher. Revising strategies can be taught, as we know from Graves (1983). Appropriate reading can be encouraged, and inappropriate models discussed. And writing teachers can learn to be patient, and silent, in the face of failures in form where the student is clearly stretching upwards.

Some of the preceding discussion, however, has raised serious questions about traditional practices in composition teaching and testing: for example, the emphasis on the writing of arguments on general subjects. We do not wish to denigrate the value of writing arguments; the structure of argument is central to academic writing as well as much public discourse. It is the locus and staging of such writing that is at issue. Perhaps the writing of arguments should be limited, at least initially, to content-area subject matter, in the context of school-sponsored learning. Alternatively, the writing of arguments in the traditional sense on topics of more personal or general concern should be staged – along the lines suggested by Dixon and Stratta (1982a). The bottom line is that it is not enough to acknowledge that students write better stories than arguments; as teachers, we must think through our practices, as well as the entire context of our students' linguistic experience, in order to understand why our students write as they do and how we can make a difference in our response.

# 8  Rediscovery of the diverse

## STEPHEN CLARKE AND JOHN SINKER

This chapter was set going by a remark that one of us made in a lecture to trainee English teachers. He said that he knew, in his classes, lots of pupils, nearly all boys, who saw 'literature' as fiction, and fiction as crinoline and chandelier stories not fit for young men. (The sexist assumption may be regrettable – but it could not be directly eradicated.) What these pupils read for preference and could be persuaded to read with ease, was travel writing, that 'notoriously raffish open house where very different genres are likely to end up in the same bed' (Raban 1987a). As it happened the other of us knew exactly what the speaker meant, and to whom he was referring, because a few months previously he had come up against that reluctance, and with the same classes, but that is another story.[1]

More significantly than for mere reminiscence, the remark began to prompt a series of thoughts that had to do with the capacity of travel writing to be discursive. If it was attractive to some pupils, for reasons to be explored later, then what was happening was that, among other genres and kinds of writing, *forms of argument* were being eagerly absorbed and, presumably, understood as, quite overtly, forms of argument. One of us had previously gone into print (Clarke 1984), regretting in public, as it were, that the reading of forms of argument was a neglected area. Yet, if travel writing could be accepted in class, and given time and sustained attention, then here was a part-solution to the problem of neglect. However, while it is probably unexceptional to claim space for travel writing somewhere within the GCSE English gamut of styles and approaches, there nevertheless seem to us a number of considerations about travel writing and pupil response to it, and to the power and place of argument within it, that need space to be developed. Our advocacy of travel writing is a tentative exploration of one way forward in the search for ways of dealing in legitimate terms with argument as a vital element within English teaching. However hard 'argument' is to define, it seems to us that, in the writings of such as Paul Theroux, James Fenton and Jonathan Raban, arguments are to hand at all points, and however much they are mingled with other intentions and effects, however much they emerge without necessarily being cast formally, their sincerity, conviction and power are what grant significance to the disparate phenomena encountered during the travel.

Both of us, as teachers, are attracted by the thought that English teaching ought to be making a considerable contribution to the 'literacy' element of 'political literacy'. It seems to us that 'English' was not always a subject that neglected political writing as a literary art – after all, an early A-level English paper (set by the JMB in 1954) contained questions on Burke's *Reflections on the French Revolution* and one of the questions addressed the nature of Burke's conservatism: in other words, it broached a directly political issue within the context of a literary study. We still welcome, and wish to encourage with students younger than those taking A levels, the notion that English can provide access to important writers whose concerns as writers, at least for part of their output, centre upon the present, public and real world every bit as much as concerns that issue in a fictional world, a place, possibility or universe that could be or might be. From here, then, it seems worth exploring how much we know about the teaching and the reading of non-fictional forms of writing. We need to ask because there already exist abundant strategies to do with teaching fiction. Yet for other forms there is less likelihood of certainty or agreement.

Literary works other than fiction, of which there are many kinds, have been absent, as examples, from nearly all the recent work aimed at English teachers on reading and response. We know far better than we did, thanks to such as Robert Protherough and David Jackson, what can happen when young readers are prompted into imaginative encounters with imaginative texts; we see how 'gaps' and picturing and testing our sense of ending can open up greater degrees of possession and inward understanding. In short, we are a good deal further advanced towards a psychology of reading fiction, and appropriate enabling strategies in our teaching. What we lack still, we think, are equivalent accounts for non-fictional texts, including texts that seek to argue, persuade and inform in ways that are not fictional ways. Equivalent accounts are required to those already gained and confirmed for novels, plays and poems. Do readers read in the same way for all kinds and genres? There has already been some dispute between the advocates of Directed Activities Relating to Texts (DARTS) for history and science texts, for example, and the English teachers working in defence of the idea of greater complexity of fiction.[2] While this seems to us a very fertile area for further empirical investigation, the presently constituted debate is in danger of polarizing the kinds of writing that pupils read and are required to read. There is a 'fact'–'fiction' division here with each area's set of supporters claiming greater difficulty and complexity for their own models, but we need to be sceptical about whether the different kinds of reading and reading-matter demanded by the curriculum polarize into neat opposites. Invisible to the dualistic view is non-fictional literature that is, nevertheless, quite unlike typical history or science writing. We need to ask what we don't yet know about how young readers read this kind of non-fictional literature, history or science. We are not entirely without pointers, however; some published work is already available about the teaching of argument, in particular an inspiring account in Horner (1983, pp. 18–26) of a whole span of learning and teaching that disregarded any formal demarcation lines between documentary and fiction, fact and rhetoric and explored by what means and to what ends you can persuade an audience of a case.

Similarly, we want to claim, travel writing disregards, in its customary forms, the same sets of demarcation lines. Travel writing invites the reader in, as it were, by devices that echo our own tentative and fragmented thinking. Our first-hand observations, partly-informed part-analyses that form the bases of our attempts to make sense of what we think we know, are given some kind of confirmation in the way that much travel writing is constructed. We are not claiming a paradigm form, but the travel writer's preparedness to be eclectic, to explore the covered territory in ways that are graphic, narrative, imaginary, discursive, reminiscent or whatever, means that the onward push of the journey demands that the things and people encountered need to be given some kind of fairly immediate evaluation, some kind of signification against the writer's view of the world. The journeys themselves, as for Theroux and Raban, might be events manufactured specifically so that a book can be made from them but the individual writer's mind, its scope and frame of reference, moral and political sensitivities, generosity or cruelty towards people encountered, all these have been constructed in advance of the journey. Part of the pleasure of the text, the enjoyment of reading travel writing may lie in seeing how far these things are modified during the course of that journey. What is more, in terms of grasp and accessibility by pupils, lots of good and exciting travel writing addresses the culturally familiar and the modern, even though it often makes it odder than it first seemed.

In these two ways, then, roughly to do with the form and content, we can see that travel writing might easily have considerable appeal for young readers whose patience with sustained fiction might be limited but who recognize in the journey both the ancient motif of adventure and knowledge, of the world and the self, and who find its varieties of form and intention, its apparently less artful inclusiveness, an echo of the sorts of thinking towards which adolescence prompts them.

There would seem, then, to be good reasons for the inclusion of travel writing among the English stock, whatever the limitations of our knowledge about how it is read. Every right-thinking English specialist advocates poetry, but the idea of prose seems to have been eclipsed, historically, by the rise of fiction as the supreme element in English teaching. It might even be claimed that the last bastion of the uncomplicated fictional novel is the English classroom. Certainly for many contemporary writers the definitional edges are substantially more blurred. Obviously this leads us into an interesting but very large area: *Flaubert's Parrot* as a class reader might be some way off but some of the best modern writing is accessible and can offer new models to a young writer.

Travel writing has a very long history, not merely as geographical record but as exploration of private and public sensibility; indeed there is plenty of landscape writing in Hardy and Dickens and so we are not trying to establish a new kind of writing that never existed before. Nevertheless, there are perhaps paradigm cases of the kinds of varied discursive writing that might repay further use in the classroom.

Bruce Chatwin's *Songlines* fuses social anthropology with a strong fictional element. Jonathan Raban frequently writes across the margins. *Coasting* is in some ways more like fiction than *Foreign Land*. Similarly autobiographical elements are found in some of V. S. Naipaul's discursive work such as *The Crocodiles of Yamoussoukro*. Comic encounters such as Clive James's *Falling Towards England* have similarly provided useful starting points for children's writing. There is a vast amount of such writing readily available.

*Soft City* by Jonathan Raban (1988) is a superb example of the fusion of observation with argument, an attempt to define modern city life qualitatively by using the tools of the novelist rather than the sociologist. There is a well-sustained quiet explosion taking place in such cross-boundary writing, writing which is fictional yet discursive and objective. Under Bill Buford's editorship, *Granta* has frequently included such work. The travel writing editions 10 and 20 are obvious starting points but so also are editions 15, 18 and 21, where there is much excellent political writing, such as James Fenton's accounts of the fall of Saigon and the revolution in the Philippines.

At the same time what we do have in the English classroom is the journal movement, with children being encouraged to write expressively: clearly the more successful and confident journals go beyond the mundane descriptions of activities and into explorations of sensibility and articulation of opinions. Now a journal writer without models is only going to know of his or her own resources but when these writers come up against other minds writing 'journals' then there are all kinds of clues, not necessarily directed, but suggested. Travel writing seems to offer such possibilities in that there are overarches to the apparently personal concerns. Something picked up at the level of individual observation is then expanded or related to something else. Theroux, discovering very poor children in South America, remembers Dr Johnson's observation that you can tell something about a country by the way it looks after its poor.

Set against this kind of fairly free writing which finds the sudden necessity for argument is the model with which we are all familiar, the 'courtroom' essay. The death of this along with the standard O-level essay seems to us to be not necessarily a bad thing. Even at Advanced level the dull marshalling of facts pro and con leads often to a sterile contactless encounter with the text. What we should like to propose, and there are huge problems associated with it, is that there is a hierarchy of discourse. At one level there is the expression of opinion and here there is a strong ludic element: the business of discussing, asserting, justifying is natural to human beings and it is only when we put a straitjacket on it that our students do not want to play.

The sense of argument that we are pursuing here either for readers or for writers is not something that is easily defined in terms of a single simple form; it is a state of mind evidenced in complex ways. There is a natural tendency – part of the game of language, part of joining the world which seeks to assert, affirm or deny – to argue back. Thus we would argue that the courtroom essay, the A-level pro and con approach, might be a premature push into too high a form of discourse: all teachers will recognize the student writing which, while conforming to the outer form, contains only inner emptiness. Dixon has started showing us that what was wrong with D- and E-grade candidates was that their writing looked as though they had never personally encountered the writing they were discussing: they may have done so, but no feeling is transmitted (Dixon and Brown 1984). It is worth remembering that one of the oldest models of education, now mistakenly considered impossibly erudite, is the form of platonic dialogue. This is a form of play with discrete voices, each voice validated by its place within the whole context, the whole community.

While such dialogue could hardly be said to be in vogue, we are witnessing an expansion in spoken argument within the English classroom through groupwork. Such groupwork at best allows the language to have just that tentative, even scruffy, exploratory feel that we know, after Britton, is so central to the learning process. Indeed it is probably the main justification for it. What is happening here is, of course, a form of discourse and this is interesting: we are recognizing it *functionally* in the classroom in an oral context but not necessarily developing it through kinds of writing which allow such space for argument to develop organically. Indeed we would go further and suggest that we have lots of good examples in the literature now of pupils talking together very seriously, offering different points of view, challenging each other at a deep and respecting level but that often there is a divorce between the spoken liveliness of argument and consequent written accounts. Maybe the links are not so hard to find as we thought.

In seeking to define a form it is interesting to observe the forms which we, as teachers, appear to find unproblematic. We are apparently confident to ask young children to take on the 'narrative' or the poetic. Yet this form we are seeking, somewhere on the continuum of assertion, opinion and argument, is what children actually do all the time. Sustained arguments which soar between the profane and the profound are not the exclusive province of our own undergraduate memories.

What these arguments, often political, have is a sense of attempted authentication of rationalization through the anecdotal form of autobiographical narrative: attempts in fact to create a kind of meaning on the world through stories exactly as we have seen observed in the writings of Harold Rosen. What follows is an attempt at creating such freedom for argument and observation through the medium of travel writing.

The challenge was to discover whether one could take the most tired theme imaginable for pupil writing, 'what I did on my holidays', and attempt to go far beyond it. Would it be possible to get travel writing as we might define it? Could the 'my holidays' writing provide a starting point for ludic argument?

By way of introduction one of us, John Sinker, read a secondary fifth-year class a variety of pieces of writing which it might be useful to outline. An obvious choice was some of the opening sections of Pirsig's novel *Zen and the Art of Motorcycle Maintenance*, where he talks about the joys of motorcycle travel *vis-à-vis* car travel and where he contrasts highways with minor roads. Also used was Clive James's account of his arrival in England in *Falling Towards England*. Here, of course, the emphasis was on humour. A selection of pieces from the travel editions of *Granta* and a piece of John Sinker's own writing were used. These pieces were intended to be funny and were really an exploration of how, when you read a travel book in a foreign country, it can modify the way you view both the writer and the place. It happened that, in *Hannibal's Footsteps* by Bernard Levin there was a lot of ludic argument, at its best a kind of extremely engaging Johnsonian pomposity. These prompted counter-observations and the wish to argue back which is what John Sinker did in his account.

So the students had been given some models but no theory or explicit instructions except that they should avoid the 'my holidays' syndrome. They all knew what was meant. What was sought was an account which would bring observation to bear on how things impinged on the young writers' own view of reality, what generalizations might come from the particulars of private experience. The young writers were told that they could certainly narrate experience as it may be formative, the anecdotal may be enlightening and thus valid, the carefully descriptive might be essential but that these forms were to be used to identify a particular view of reality.

Here is one response:

> The waitress bent down to wipe the table. She had a cloth in her right hand which she circled around the table in quick, light movements. Then she reached over towards some empty glasses by the side of the table.
>
> The glasses were a mixture: of tall straight glasses with many melting ice cubes and curious objects like mini-umbrellas and multi-coloured straws and flags inside them, wine glasses instantly recognizable by their round shapes standing on thin tubes of glass leading towards their bases, and most abundant of all forty beer glasses, no ice, no straws, no umbrellas.
>
> The waitress looked at them in a curiously affectionate manner. She gave a sigh as she reached out and picked them up, clutching them between fingers and thumbs so that each one pushed on another one's sides.
>
> A lot can be learned from a pile of empty glasses if you are willing to look close enough: Who was drinking from them. How many there was in the group. Their taste. Their budget.
>
> With the glasses in tight grasp she made her way back to the bar. In doing so she had to brush past groups of young men, standing with glasses in their hands; they were all drinking, smoking, laughing, joking. Without attracting any wolf-whistles or any groping hands she skilfully crossed the room. Quite noticeably this was not easy, it looked like a highly practised skill, as if this barmaid valued herself too highly to flirt with customers just to persuade them to come again.
>
> As a barmaid she seemed out of place. She was obviously a local. Her brown eyes and straight dark hair gave her naturally creamy sunned skin a subtlety that so acutely was lacking in tanned foreigners whose two week colour change so harshly

contrasts with their features and hair. She wore no make up. No tarty clothes and was very quiet. The pub however wore make up: modern decorating, green walls, artificial plants, framed prints on the walls, a glass case with a display of jumpers and ties for sale, a 'video juke-box' that created more noise and chaos than even that of the clients.

At the bar she pressed a small glass on an upturned bottle. The glass filled and she turned, to accept, over the counter, some light coins and an old note in exchange. She reached over and the man at the other side of the bar smiled. She smiled back. Her smile was cold and radiated none of the emotions that the man had hoped for. He scuttled away and disappeared into the crowds instead of sitting at the bar as he planned.

She opened a till and placed in it the note; the coins went into her pocket.

Behind her was an open doorway in which a man stood blocking out the view behind him. He flew into a rage. His eyes were bulging out of his dark weathered skin. He darted to where she was and began to shake his finger at her as he spoke to her in Greek. She ran off towards the doorway crying and wiping her eyes on her blouse arm.

Through the open doorway a door slammed. The man, who it was now apparent was the owner took over the girl's job and began to serve drinks. He did this with authority that set him worlds apart from the girl's uninvolved cold manner. He chatted to his customers as he took their money he was warm friendly, but somehow he seemed artificial – switching from reprimanding the girl to make small talk over the bar was done with an unhidden degree of professionalism.

Now the girl had gone and the man was serving drinks I could see right into the hallway beyond the bar. It was a telling scene: a bare light bulb hung from a white ceiling full of cracks, dust and squashed mosquitoes. There was a telephone – large, old fashioned and black – leading from one corner of the room to another by a pile of washing. The floors were concrete and there was a large door, obviously not in use at the end of the doorway near a staircase with more dirty washing piled against it like a pile of glasses in a bar – you can tell a lot from a pile of washing if you look carefully.

Everything fell together in that moment. These were real people conducting real lives in their homes. But outside, in the bar, these people were in a false environment created by themselves out of need. The bar was a different world from the one in the hallway. The man who had done well and seemed to be the owner had the ability to cope with this, he had adapted well. The girl was a different kind of person. She had not adapted well to the false world of the bar. It is not necessary to say she is not good at putting on an act and that the man is. It would be more accurate to say that she is unwilling to put on an act. She tries to live her life whilst at work. The man had sacrificed this in order to live a better life outside it, in coping with his work he lives better, whereas the girl can not see this.

How awful I thought, that these people must fit with the clients rather than the clients making an effort to fit in with the natural environment of the foreign bar staff. Surely the people standing around drinking would benefit from the experience of getting to know real locals, being real in a real part of a foreign country. But this would require effort. The effort to be patient, to submit to foreign cultures and perhaps even to make an attempt to understand their language rather than have everyone speaking to them in English. This was clearly impossible, I thought, as I looked around the pub. It was these people who were forcing the locals to be false. I was one of them, this worried me. This had been the year when I had hoped to make the effort. My German was at the point where, perhaps, I could be understood without demanding that I should be spoken to in English, my French was such that I reasonably could have tried to be inconspicuous. But Greece? I've heard of 'pi' in maths, 'alpha', 'gamma', 'delta', and 'rho' in physics but this was hardly much of a start.

I stood up to go. I thought to myself that you can learn a lot from languages. Like empty glasses and dirty washing. Take German, isn't it just so obvious what kind of a nation they are simply by listening to their language? As I understand it the stereotype typical German is supposed to be calculated, well planned, strong and forceful, now I wouldn't claim for one minute that this is a fair representation; I don't know many Germans but I'm sure, many of them are as compassionate as the Italian race are said to be. But can't you see my point, when I say that the language of a country fits the stereotype of the people? Perhaps the stereotypes do not emerge from meeting people out from their language. Or perhaps the shape of the language shapes the people, after all we all think in our own language so perhaps this can affect personality. Could the subordinating conjunctions, separable prefixes, strong verbs, strict word order and punctuation rules sending verbs all over the place in the German language lead to the better manufacturing of quality precision cars? Could the round endings on Italian words and their flowing style of speech lead to compassionate understanding of human love? Could the Americans' 'think big' strategy have led from the way they pronounce their vowels? It seems a reasonable conclusion to draw. It is much fairer to group nationalities together than colours. After all people of the same nationality share, not only language but also culture, way of life and in many cases religion. Whereas no matter what the colour of your skin, in this day and age, you could have been raised anywhere, without any connection to one country. Even if stereotypes are fair (which they probably are not) there is no valid case for making an evaluation due to colour.

Ian's piece seems to us to be particularly well thought through and complete. He starts from close observation of bar glasses and develops a sensitive, reflective response through, among other things, an ironic detached repetition. The full force is achieved only in the final sentence. It makes interesting reading in conjunction with the following, by Jonathan Raban (1987b):

The best place to commit suicide in north London is from the top of the Archway Bridge, a magnificently vulgar piece of Victorian ironwork that carries Hornsey Lane high over the top of Archway Road. Your death leap will cast you from the precarious gentility of N.6 into the characterless squalor of N.19. All Highgate trembles on the edge of that abyss, perched, like a gentlewoman of rapidly reducing means, above the 'vapid plains' of that 'hot and sickly odour of the human race which makes up London'. Highgate was firmly behind the 19th-century rector of Hornsey, Canon Harvey, who declared (in a letter to *The Times*): 'I have tried to keep Hornsey a village but circumstances have beaten me.' It was always a place for prospects and dreams of the city lying below it: Dick Whittington turned again on Highgate Hill; Guy Fawkes's cronies gathered in Parliament Hill Fields to watch the Houses of Parliament blaze. Then it became an escape hatch, as the middle classes built their purple brick villas like castles on the northern heights, in defence against the cholera and typhoid germs of William Booth's Darkest London. N.6 is an embattled vantage point; it overlooks the city with a chronic mixture of anticipation and fear.

Despite obvious differences, what we sense here is a confident willingness to engage in the complex business not only of observing the world but reacting to it and seeking explanation for how things come to be as they are. Such writing is not in any way antithetical to creative engagement, indeed it is predicated upon it. Just as Raban does, Ian seeks to register discontinuities between the self and the world. The fact that his strategy is at this point more definitely reliant on individual admission in no way invalidates the effectiveness of the attempt; indeed, much has been learned by our young writer about the power achieved in writing when the subjective stance contains contrary voices.

Other young writers achieved a level of honesty and critical reflection on the mundanities of holiday travel. Alison Bown wrote of a car journey through France:

I found the landscape uninteresting and generally rather dull. Looking out I watched the fields moving, blurring into each other, colours running to grey. And it was still raining. Perpetual. The French climate had failed. I noticed my sister, curled up in the corner of the car sulking. I was interested to find out if she was sulking because of the weather (like myself, only I'm more discreet) or because her walkman had broken down. I ask. The reply? A uncomprehensible mass of four-letter words. Dad raised an eyebrow. I shrank back and continued my quest for something interesting to look at amongst the grey. The climate had failed rather ignominiously on the travel brochure's behalf. Predictably it was the first rain of the summer season. Britain followed us everywhere: in the form of pasty faced tourists, prejudice and, of course, the weather (we got four decent days from the entire holiday). I closed my eyes and dreamed of summer.

Later in her piece Alison became more introspective.

Parents were a problem, a bind on my freedom. I wanted, yearned to explore. Instead I got deadlines and their constant companionship. I like being on my own, even thrive on it. Being with any group of people in a tent for two weeks, with no real escape, troubles me. The fact that it was my parents made no difference, except they were a hand of authority. I cannot tell ANYBODY where to go, I clam up anyway so it wasn't the fact I couldn't argue with my parents. I guess that for most of the time while we go on holiday together, I dislike my mum and dad. It's sad and it clouded the holiday.

David Buncall's piece, again recapturing a car journey through France, starts off in a more ebullient tone but again there is sustained reflection and interesting comment:

Now 'a la France', one pays for the privilege of driving on the motorways. The excuse for this is that the money goes towards maintaining the roads. But this is fairly confusing as French autoroutes (along with the one through the Amazon Rain forest) have to go down as some of the worst Motorways in the world. Our opinion is that they spend so much on the expensive hi-tech toll booths that they don't have beaucoup de centimes left to spend on actual road maintenance.

The trick to driving on these motorways is to take your GB sticker off. GB seems to be a challenge to all the numerous potential Alain Prosts in their Renault 129.5's to scream up behind the caravan, hooting and flashing and giving varied bi-digital gestures. This can be very infuriating as you're trying to overtake the knackered Dutch Volkswagen camper that's chugging along in front.

The comic tone established, David's account of travelling through Lyon contains a recognizable truth behind the deliberate extravagance.

All those who've passed their French Level 1 driving exam are now confronted with the ultimate in driving experiences. Lyon is a grotty, huge, ugly, belching, industrial zit in the middle regions of France. The road system through Lyon is devised so that whatever time of year/day/night there is always a ten mile traffic jam. Cars exceeding the ten mile limit are run into by a speeding BMW.

Being veterans of an earlier campaign and sporting 'I've visited Lyon' stickers on the back of the van to prove it, we were well equipped with the survival kit (2 days of food and drink, sleeping bags, and plenty of tips to give to the array of buskers playing along the queue). It amazes me how the inhabitants put up with it. I've seen people letting their houses out to people in the queue. You also have the opportunity to make life long friends with the people next to you in the queue (if you're unlucky they will be Italian terrorists but if you're not you can become quite attached).

These extracts are part of an interesting piece. One is here engaged with an intelligence, a detached persona whose fortunes and whose sense of the absurd and ridiculous one shares. Later he moves on to make some interesting generalizations about the British abroad and travel by ferry. However, we are not unaware here of the problem of presenting an unconscious model. In retrospect, it seems that the prior readings given to the class were overloaded towards the humorous. Furthermore, the fact that John Sinker's own piece adopted in parts a comic postcard tone may have unduly influenced some of the writing which came out of the group. This is always a problem. Perhaps David caught his teacher's own tendency to bombast but, on the other hand, there is an obligation, we believe, on us teachers to be engaged in a shared struggle to create writing, to share the raid on the inarticulate. Perhaps simultaneous creation would be better, but that is a counsel of perfection.

The emphasis we would wish to make in this writing is that it can provide a means of achieving many of the things that the rhetoric claims for fiction. The compulsion to understand and make shape of the immediate is certainly to be found in many novels but to use only fiction seems to us to be unnecessarily limiting. And, of course, we need to remember that young readers may not see in what sense novels are generated from the writer's sense of immediate engagement with the world. Aidan Chambers tells us of how when first encountering *Sons and Lovers* he was delivered from his sense of being alone in the world. The writing we have considered can achieve this sense of community and otherness precisely because it starts from a confident sense of selfhood.

What we are not seeking is any kind of contest with fiction, nor are we attempting a kind of fashionable tough-mindedness over the place of discursive writing in the English classroom. We are attempting, by recognizing a hierarchy of discourse, to add to the range of empathetic and discursive possibility. Travel writing offers just such opportunities.

## Acknowledgement

We are grateful to Collins Harvill Ltd. for permission to quote from Jonathan Raban's *For Love and Money*.

## Notes

1  The authors swapped jobs for the spring term of 1987, Clarke teaching Sinker's classes in school and Sinker supervising Clarke's PGCE English students on teaching practice.
2  See Protherough (1987, pp. 82–3), where he disputes with Davies and Greene (1984) about whether it is true, as the latter claim, that science texts require more careful and reflective reading than the more easily 'received' fictions offered in English.

# 9 Developing argument at sixteen plus

JUDITH ATKINSON

> I hope I have managed to convey my opinions in a straightforward and balanced way and not with a self-righteous attitude. When I set out to write this assignment I had so much I wanted to express but sometimes it is difficult to actually write down on paper what is in your mind. Well, I gave it a try anyway! (Kirsty)

It is not surprising that Kirsty at sixteen finds it difficult 'to actually write down on paper' her opinions and evaluations, particularly when she has set herself the task of conveying them in a 'balanced way' and without a 'self-righteous attitude'. To present a reasoned case with both commitment and objectivity is a daunting task for a young writer. During a two-year GCSE course Kirsty has given lively and unselfconscious accounts of her own experience in talking and writing, and has handled different kinds of fictional writing with confidence. In her journal she has told the story of her reading during the course in fluent jottings which combine expressions of feeling and thought. Why is it, then, that an invitation to express views on a chosen topic undermines her usual confidence? One answer is that this sixteen-year-old in her honesty recognizes that she is still too young to have firmly formed 'opinions'. She is feeling and thinking intensely, as her phrase 'I had so much I wanted to express' suggests, but the discipline, as she perceives it, of giving ordered written expression to that press of responses has in some way changed their nature: 'I *had* so much I wanted to express'. By the end of the assignment she expresses disappointment because the struggle to give a final and polished set of views has somehow diminished the urgency of the original feelings and thoughts.

A second answer may be that Kirsty sees the writing task she has taken on as in a genre which is totally different from the other kinds of writing she has successfully done during the course. Unlike stories or journal entries, this is to be 'straightforward' and 'balanced'. She believes the style and tone should be clear and cool and the structure somehow a representation of a weighing-up process. This final paragraph of her attempt to write in such a way suggests that she has had to struggle to give an alien kind of order to the raw material 'in (her) mind'.

Kirsty's struggles to handle written argument are similar to those experienced by many sixteen-year-old writers. Yet for many years examiners and, therefore, teachers expected pupils of this age to 'convey opinions' in the constricting circumstances of an end-of-course O-level or CSE English Language examination. Several factors combined to add further difficulties to those expressed by Kirsty. The writing was to be carried out in a limited time, with no opportunity for drafting and rethinking. Opinions were asked for on controversial topics but candidates had no access to information material or alternative views. Perhaps most importantly, adult examiners proposed the topics for writing, giving a choice, but always a restricted one, and, through the wording of titles and questions, making it clear that a precise genre was expected. A brief historical analysis of such questions reveals the difficulty and artificiality of the writing tasks set for Kirsty's predecessors.

Representative of O-level English Language papers from the 1950s is the Cambridge 1957 paper which presents the following instruction and stimuli for discursive or argument-style writing:

> Write a composition on one of the following subjects:
> Getting and spending.
> A world without oil.
> T.V. as a means of entertainment and instruction.
> 'A woman's place is in the home'.

In this list the topics are unpromising because they are either generalized or conventional. The assumption underlying the framing of the questions is that candidates should be capable of bringing, from a baldly simple stimulus, feelings and thoughts into being, of giving them a coherent shape and of expressing them clearly and cogently – all in given time limit. They are in reality an invitation to word-spinning.

In 1971 a West Midlands CSE paper, despite making an attempt to offer topics with a nearer relevance to sixteen-year-olds and a simpler instruction, gives as little encouragement and help to candidates.

> Choose just one title and write it at the top of your composition.
> Hooliganism.
> Teenage fashions.
> Some of the changes going on around us today.

In 1973 a JMB paper shows that examiners are beginning to acknowledge that candidates have individuality and that *their* views will be welcomed and given credit:

> What are your views on 'Women's Lib.'?

The assumption is still, however, that such 'views' can be neatly formulated and are worth writing.

By 1978 the framing of some questions reflects the influence of early coursework practices and shows an awareness that sixteen-year-olds need stimulus and material for thought if they are to write with any kind of personal authority. The following JMB question makes a clear contrast with the earlier CSE title 'Hooliganism'.

> Violence and vandalism are common in our society. Various reasons are suggested for this: loss of influence of the church, certain programmes on T.V., lack of parental control, boredom, lack of effective punishment in school and in the courts, general attitude of the nation, alcohol, drugs. What do you think are the causes and what do you suggest could be done about the problem?

Yet the artificiality of the writing task is still present. The leads given in this question are still the examiner's, and the candidates' role is to reorganize and express in their own terms someone else's material.

This approach to question-framing is extended and given some openness in pilot sixteen-plus papers for NEA in which candidates are given a page of source material and then asked to 'discuss *some* of the points raised, adding points of your own to develop your argument'.

Bearing in mind the apparent reasons for Kirsty's difficulties with argument-writing it is not surprising that the majority of answers in this genre proved disappointing to examiners: 'The organising of thoughts into coherent paragraphs and the construction of a well ordered argument continued to give difficulty to many candidates. As usual in this section, there were also many short, undeveloped answers.'[1] Given little choice of topic, many candidates found themselves writing on issues to which they had no genuine response. Unable to research material or exchange experiences in talk many fell back on empty assertion: 'Many otherwise well written essays relied rather heavily on assertion without supportive evidence – an approach that resulted in a rather thin quality to the writing.'[2] Writing for an unknown examiner and for no perceivable purpose other than passing the exam, candidates often produced essays which, in examiners' words, 'tended to lack conviction'.[3]

Since 1986, GCSE syllabuses for all the existing examining boards have maintained the requirement for candidates of all abilities to 'produce and sustain argument, to handle and present ideas', in the words of NEA Syllabus B. Some have preserved the O-level/CSE practice of making a sharp distinction between argument and other kinds of writing, particularly narrative. Others have taken the important step of recognizing the unhelpfulness for pupils at this stage of development of making artificial classifications of writing. NEA Syllabus B, for example, gives the following advice to teachers.

> These are *not* to be taken as five rigid or predetermined categories of writing. Much of the work done by candidates will show evidence of more than one of the aspects of writing identified for assessment. For example – a persuasive piece on education may include personal narrative as illustration.[4]

Although this statement is promising, it fails to go far enough. Narrative is still seen as illustration, a supportive reference to the line of thought rather than an integral part of the whole texture of the writing.

Given both this understanding on some examiners' part of the close relationship between argument and narrative, and the enhanced opportunities for writing presented by coursework, what have the first generation of GCSE pupils achieved as writers of argument? As an attempt to answer the question, what follows is a picture of several writers at the end of their GCSE English and Literature courses. As one of their final pieces of coursework they have been asked to explore their views on any topic about which they have strong feelings. Nothing has been laid down about structure or style; pupils are free to approach the writing in their own chosen way. As an exercise in discussing and evaluating source material, and to provide a starting point for pupils who declare that they have 'no strong feelings about anything', the class have watched and discussed two television programmes showing children's varied experiences of education and in groups have used prompt questions to start them on evaluation of their own school experience.

Christine is one of the pupils who has chosen to give her 'views on education'. In her opening paragraph she declares an ambitious intention 'to show the British education as it is today, what is intended for the future and my own education and views'. An extract from her account of her own education will give the flavour of the whole piece.

> My primary school gave me a sound basic knowledge before progressing to secondary school. The first years of my secondary education prepared me for work in my final two years before external examinations. It has taught me how to use my time, what is expected of me and the sort of work I would be studying in the future. My education has also given me the knowledge I will need as an adult in all aspects of life.

After the stimulus of two hotly-debated TV programmes and lively group discussion of past experiences and their significance, Christine's written response is disappointing. She is giving the teacher what she imagines the teacher wants, both in her expressed attitudes and in her adopted style – despite the fact that the teacher has not expressed any precise expectations. Her catalogue of what she has gained from education reads like the official 'Aims of the school' and the vocabulary – 'sound basic', 'progressing', 'expected of me', 'knowledge I will need' – seems to echo the lifeless official wording of official government documents about education. She reveals a mechanistic view of the system that 'gave me', 'prepared me' and 'taught me'. It is difficult to believe that the 'I' she is writing about is really Christine because the impersonal tone disengages her from her subject matter. Her insecurity with her adopted mode of writing makes itself clear in the use of paragraphs and in the clumsy sentence structures.

By comparison, Hayley, choosing the same topic, accepts the invitation to 'explore' and in the course of a long assignment considers a wide range of issues. Here she is writing about the programme she has watched, her experience of infant school and of GCSE.

Before being accepted at the school at five Georgia has undergone an exam which she had to pass. Once struggling over the first hurdle there is then an army-like fashion in which the teachers conduct the class. The girls will all stand as if posing for a school photograph and recite words from the board.

My younger days were spent learning basic things such as: reading and writing. But at the same time the teachers offered us a range of activities in the classroom once you'd completed a certain subject – the playhouse or the sandpit. It was rather like us being blackmailed due to us finishing the work and then being able to choose our favourite toy, which evidently worked. 'Continual assessment' is a little misleading. I believed it would be a report each quarter of the year by the teachers to tell moderators how we were progressing in our class and homework. Maybe that was a little wishful thinking! But as I discussed before, in primary and lower school our lessons were much more exciting and interesting but now all that seems to be enjoyable is the debates and discussions in English. All the other lessons – the syllabus is drummed into our head and then we copy it up for homework – the only thing that they want to do is drill everything into us as fast as they can to finish the syllabus, which we can all understand, but why not make it a little more interesting?

Hayley would not satisfy the previously quoted examiners, as this is not a 'well ordered argument'. Unlike Christine, however, she is expressing her own views and experiences directly and vigorously, and, although it is never made explicit in the assignment, she does make clear her picture of how education should be. Through the retelling of the three sets of experience quoted in the extracts above, she shows that she believes education should be active and enjoyable and that teachers should be enablers rather than instructors. In the first extract the lively images of regimentation carry the idea, as does the comparison with 'blackmail' to describe a teacher's effective methods with young children. In the final paragraph 'interesting', 'exciting' and 'enjoyable' are set against 'drummed' and 'drill . . . as fast as they can'.

Where Hayley seems to discover her own views in the process of writing, Kathy comes to the topic of education having thought out her position already, as she states firmly at the beginning of the assignment,

The following report is probably very biassed, but as the title says, these are MY views on education and they probably don't match anybody else's ideas.

This might seem like the introduction to a series of unsubstantiated prejudices, but this is not Kathy's way. In considering a range of issues she brings in the television programmes and points made by her friends in discussion to weigh up against her own views, in the process either modifying or strengthening her original position. Recalling the programmes, for example, helps her to give expression to views about the nature of teachers and teaching and confirms her dislike of the competitive element in education.

At Rugby school the 'Masters' were people to look up to and be afraid of. There was even a military training lesson. Before going to Liverpool, the Rugby pupils were told to look out for 'left wing gay libbers'. I certainly don't agree at all to the way the teachers at Rugby preached their politics. The pupils should be left to find out for themselves about politics in order to form their own opinions. I don't suppose for a moment that all public schools take this attitude towards politics, but it is something which struck me in the documentary. In the 'Citizen 2000' video we saw how a young girl called Georgia was taught at her public school. It certainly seemed to be all work and no play. Children cannot be expected to learn facts in the 'parrot fashion' that these five year olds were learning to spell, children need to be motivated and the style in which Georgia was learning things certainly wouldn't motivate me. . . . I couldn't help noticing that when Georgia's mother was talking to her about school, she only seemed concerned about who was best in the class at reading and who was the cleverest. I don't feel that being the best at everything is at all important. As long as the pupil is performing to the best of his or her ability, that is all that should matter.

Kathy makes three thoughtful points in this extract and the process of thought and expression is similar each time. She was 'struck' by the words of the Rugby teacher, prepares for explicit comment on it with her word 'preached' and is then able to state with confidence that she disagrees with teaching as indoctrination. Georgia's lesson is described, judged implicitly in the phrase 'parrot fashion', and emphatically dismissed in the light of Kathy's own experience. In a similar way she 'couldn't help noticing' Georgia's mother's conversation, judges it with the phrase 'only seemed concerned' and finishes with a clear statement of her own feeling.

Pupils who chose their own topics to explore were not able to draw on recent shared experiences in the same way as Hayley and Kathy. They were, however, reminded of the way in which source material and memories of personal experience had been built up during preparation for writing about education and were encouraged to use research, interviewing and remembering as part of their own preparation.

Erica's writing about abortion provides an example of the difficulties a sixteen-year-old faces in tackling a complex topic which by its nature often provokes strong feeling rather than patient thought. She strikes this note in her introductory paragraph.

The controversial subject of abortion is one I feel very strongly about. It isn't just the fact that I am Roman Catholic although of course that is partly it but I would have the same feelings whatever religion I was.

This sets the tone for the rest of the assignment which is carried along by a series of emphatic and vigorous statements of belief. She expresses hesitancy only once,

In Cases of Rape I'm undecided, if the girl/woman becomes pregnant after being raped I'm not sure what should be done.

The following paragraph is more characteristic.

Even in the first few weeks of pregnancy the tiny blob of cells is alive, it will develop into a tiny human being and women say 'It's not a baby at that stage, it isn't alive'. Pathetic. Of <u>course</u> it's alive, those cells are developing all the time and it is alive . . .

how can women have the life scraped out of them and not feel absolutely grief-stricken and ashamed for the rest of their lives? . . . Frankly I am sickened by such views. It just isn't a matter of how many weeks pregnant you are, that blob of cells is ALIVE.

The urgency with which Erica feels her case is there in the language – the terse 'Pathetic.', the emotive 'scraped out of them' and the underlining and final capitals. The assignment reads like a speech and it is ironic that it is written by the shyest and most reticent member of the class. Also present in the extract is Erica's inability to recognize or empathize with the alternative case, shown in her amazement and disgust at women who justify or have had abortions. The assignment draws on statistics and the results of interviews but what gives it its drive is its certainty. An adult reader would probably question whether this certainty is genuinely Erica's.

Kirsty, whose final paragraph formed the starting point of *this* essay, is impelled by a strength of feeling similar to Erica's as she considers 'Divisions in Society'. At one point she writes:

I sit, like I am sure many other people do, and cry when I watch the news pictures on T.V. that stare at me. But most of all I ask why?

In a consciously shaped assignment she explores 'the "North/South divide"', religious differences, colour prejudice and the inequalities between rich and poor countries. She sets out her aim in simple terms at the beginning.

I realise that by writing this assignment I am not going to suddenly right any of the wrongs there are in the world or change anything, it is merely a way to express my own opinions on this subject.

Where Erica has used her writing for a piece of polemic, Kirsty is consciously setting out to use hers as a vehicle to explore and come to terms with her feelings and thoughts. She soon reveals herself as a sixteen-year-old idealist saddened, bewildered and frustrated by the world which confronts her. What is unusual in a writer of her age is the balance she maintains throughout. She acknowledges and considers alternative viewpoints, admits her own ignorance, expresses bewilderment and powerlessness honestly but has the confidence to trust the rightness of her own instincts and reactions. Characteristic of the whole assignment is the following extract.

There is one more division which angers me. There is a war going on between government and communists in Africa which is resulting in innocent bystanders starving to death. Supplies of food are not able to get through to these people because of someone else's problem. I realise there are facts I don't understand but what I do understand and what I do see is men, women and children starving to death and I think it is disgusting that in 1988 there are millions of people without food. I don't care what reasons governments give, nothing on earth justifies those people's pain, and what makes it worse is that the EEC has 'mountains' and 'lakes' of unwanted food – tonnes of grain, sitting uselessly . . . Why should anyone today have to starve to death? I am sure I will wait a long time for that answer.

Tom and Sally, whose work will be considered next, both choose to present their views in the more traditional 'debating style' form but there are interesting differences between them.

Although Tom's commitment to his chosen topic is not in doubt, his writing about capital punishment has the feel of an intellectual exercise. He is trying on a style of thinking and writing and his assignment makes a striking contrast with the personal directness of Kirsty's. Here he is pursuing one of the points in his case:

> Isn't it cheaper for the state to execute a prisoner than to keep him or her imprisoned for life? This last question is typical of the people who seem to think that human life can be compared with economics, and want to see the return of capital punishment. If a money value could be used, I would put up the counter attack that equally costly would be the mass court cases, appeals, not even mentioning solicitors' or judges' fees. Thus the death penalty can be extremely costly as a punishment form in view of all the elaborate procedures that are carried out, especially with efforts involved to minimize the possibility of an irreversible error.

Tom is consciously debating his case – framing the question from imagined opponents – 'people who seem to think that human life can be compared with economics' – then presenting his own answer in the debating arena, his 'counter attack'. He has chosen vocabulary and sentence structures that he considers appropriate; 'elaborate procedures', 'minimize the possibility', 'if a money value could be used, I would put up . . .', 'Thus'.

Sally debates a topic about which she has first-hand knowledge and experience. She is a member of Greenpeace and has been involved in its campaign to put a stop to whale-hunting. Here she recounts local moves to organize a boycott of Icelandic fish after 'physical' moves against the country's 'barbaric whaling' have had only limited success.

> Greenpeace set about organising their boycott by sending postcards out to their local supermarket. The card explained about the boycott and asked the super-market to either stop selling Icelandic fish or to clearly label its origin. I have seen a reply from Sainsburys' customer relations department. The letter says that they have been asked before, on numerous occasions to boycott products both for moral and political reasons. They put forward the very reasonable argument that they do not feel it is right to impose decisions on their customers. I agree with them on this point – that it is indeed the consumer's decision. So they cannot stop selling Icelandic fish, but why then can they not label their products clearly? Sainsburys also have an argument against this, they say it is impossible because the fish markets they use are, in their turn, supplied by boats 'registered in a variety of countries'. They compromise by giving a vague guidance as to the origin of the fish, e.g. 'Fished in North Atlantic Waters'. If this is true then why is it possible for some stores, e.g. Marks and Spencers to be able to say that none of their fish is Icelandic?

By comparison with Tom's assignment, Sally's reads easily because it is written clearly, fluently and with the confidence of knowledge. She writes like a practised arguer, which she has been for two years in class discussion, but she is also in a real debate. Where Tom had to invent adversaries Sally's tenacious argument is with Sainsburys. She is able maturely to acknowledge the 'reasonable' argument she has been given but refuses to be fobbed off, posing another question and coming back persistently when that, too, is evaded.

Julia begins her assignment 'Quantity or Quality' as though she is going to write a narrative account of her Work Experience week in the geriatric ward at a local hospital. After describing the room and individual patients she writes this:

> The main aim of the doctors there seemed to be to prolong the patient's life for as long as possible. Quite a few did make a full recovery, but there were several people there who seemed to be making no real progress at all. There was one man who was so dehydrated that he had to be put onto a drip. This was originally fitted to his lower arm, but the veins there kept collapsing, so it had to be moved to the upper arm. I watched the ward doctor do this. I stood in the little ward off the main corridor containing just the one bed, watching him as he tried several times to get the needle into the vein, which stood proud of the wretched-looking arm. Each time he made a fresh attempt I heard the poor man give a little grunt of pain and I felt nauseated by the smell of the sickly 'vanilla build-up' that the nurses had been feeding him on.
>
> His condition deteriorated during the week I was there, and on the Friday I found out that he wasn't expected to live until the morning. 'They'll still try and revive him you know', a nurse said to me. This really shocked me, because even if they succeeded in keeping him alive, how long would it be for, and what sort of life would he have, lying moaning on a bed all day with a needle stuck in his arm?
>
> I realise that you can't just let somebody die, you have to give them some kind of treatment with drugs or whatever, because in many cases there is a future for the patient involved. I also realise that it would be very difficult for a doctor to know where to draw the line. It's just that in this man's case the lengths they went to seemed to me to be extreme and pointless.

Like Sally, Julia is writing with the confidence of experience. When she questions the medical ethics of artificially prolonging old people's lives she is not arguing a hypothetical case and her final statement has weight because her story of the dying man has led the reader to share her growing feelings of disgust, compassion and shock. Despite the strength of her feeling she is able to acknowledge the arguments of the alternative view and to realize in her final sentence that she can only make a statement about the particular case and that it would be wrong to generalize from that.

So what are the achievements of these sixteen-year-old writers and of the GCSE approach?

1 Pupils like Christine can still write in the lifeless way O-level examiners would recognize, but the rest write with life because they have something they want to communicate.
2 The range of approaches is interesting – each finding a form and style appropriate to his or her own topic and intention.

3  Most express their individuality – except perhaps Tom, who is practising a style.
4  With the advantages of time and writing for a known reader most have avoided merely asserting a case. They have chosen issues they can explore with authority.
5  For many of them the authority comes from experience and expresses itself in writing which cannot be categorized just as 'argument'. Julia's is the clearest example of writing which moves between argument and narrative and gains its power from that.

## Notes

1  *GCE Examiners' Reports 1986*, Manchester: Joint Matriculations Board Examinations Council.
2  *Report on the 1987 Examination, Joint GCE O-Level and CSE Examinations, English Syllabuses A and B*, Manchester: NEA.
3  *GCE Examiners' Reports 1986*, Manchester: JMB.
4  *GCSE English Syllabus B, Syllabus for the 1988 examination*, Manchester: NEA.

# 10 Persuading as storying: essays, narrative rhetoric and the college writing course

## DOUGLAS HESSE

The field of college writing instruction seems not quite to know what to do with narrative. The 1986 publication of Judith and Geoffrey Summerfield's *Texts and Contexts*, marked by its receiving the Modern Language Association's Mina Shaughnessy Prize, offers a dramatic sign of narrative's newly-recognized role in undergraduate composition courses. Perhaps more dominant, however, are contentions that narrative is too simple, too literary, and, most significantly, too 'impractical' to merit serious attention in college writing and rhetoric classrooms.[1] Those charges, however, manifest two significant misunderstandings, one of the personal essay, the other of how narrative persuades. This chapter will address mainly the second concern by means of the first. In other words, I will show how understanding the use of stories in personal essays leads to a more general theory of the rhetoric of narrative. This rhetoric governs works beyond personal essays, even ones which do not contain 'stories' in the usual sense of the term.

The result is an argument for narrative couched in terms beyond the traditional rationales. To be specific, my argument does not rest on narrative as 'an easier, first mode' for young writers. It does not rest on narrative as the best means for developing 'voice'. It does not rest on narrative as the best way to teach students the importance of detail. It does not rest on narrative as a way to introduce the concept of 'thesis' through an Aesop's-Fables-like attachment of meaning to experience. Instead, my argument for narrative rests on its function as a powerful persuasive strategy, one which derives force not from hierarchical logic but from the emplotment of propositions. To put this another way, I suggest shifting our attention from narrative as a type of proof to narrative as a form of argument. To put it a third way, I argue that the best classical account of the persuasive effect of narrative in non-fictional texts is not Aristotle's *Rhetorica* but his *De Poetica*, especially the *Poetics* as read by Paul Ricoeur.

This chapter will synthesize elements of current literary and rhetorical theory to characterize the rhetoric of narrative. It is divided into three sections. The first summarizes and corrects some traditional dismissals of narrative in writing classes and some traditional misunderstandings of the function of narrative in personal essays. The second explains how narrative persuades. The third discusses implications of this narrative rhetoric for the future of the personal essay, for discourse analysis and for writing and reading instruction.

## Toward a truer view of narrative in essays

In the ongoing pedagogical battles between teaching experiential writing and teaching expository/rhetorical writing, champions of the latter make two main arguments. The first, an economic one, assumes the scarcity of personal narrative both in other academic settings and in that golden 'real world' of work after college. Storytelling is dismissed as a largely belletristic exercise that deprives students of writing more apparently susceptible to financial reward. The second, more serious challenge, comes from a different quarter. This charge is that overemphasizing narrative inhibits intellectual growth because it privileges a simplistic mode of cognition. Narrative is 'natural' or 'unavoidable', the argument begins. Because we narrate all of the time yet we do not naturally construct systematic analyses and syntheses of written texts, the latter activities are more significant to college writing curricula. This argument lies beyond economics, its justification the loftier one of cognitive development. Summerfield and Summerfield (1986, p. 102) have characterized the dismissal that has resulted: 'In the teaching of composition, we have tended to bypass narrative, to relegate it to a step along the way to more complex forms, particularly to exposition. Narrative is generally seen as a "simple" mode'. Others scarcely grant narrative status even as a step. Mike Rose (1983, p. 115) summarizes work that finds 'academic expositional discourse' to be 'more cognitively demanding than simple narration or description', and he cautions that even preliminary studies 'should make us wary of assuming that mastering, say, narrative structure will enable students to construct analytic essays'.

Combined, these two arguments pose a serious challenge. If classroom narratives appear to bear no resemblance to real world writing (which often means writing directly susceptible to financial reward), and if writing them appears to contribute little to developing real world skills, what place do they have in writing classes, especially when aesthetic or personal growth rationales are out of favour?

At the very least, the first argument breaks down with the understanding that narrative does not equal autobiography. I would concede that *if* freshman writing textbooks at all reflect current classroom practice, the kinds of narrative essay written by students do not resemble, even in kind, writing beyond the classroom.

In the name of essaying, teachers often require students to search their pasts for stories, write them, then state their meaning by attaching a thesis. The thesis is always about the narrative, must always circumscribe it somehow, and must appear in a several-sentence introduction or conclusion. Notice the conflicting signals this gives students, who are simultaneously asked to contract everything to a point and to expand that point into a paragraph, at least, that accompanies the story. The frustrations inherent to this situation are clear. When a single statement can say what the story means, who can fault students' inability to supply extra words? More rarely, teachers have students work in the other direction, searching their pasts for a story that will prove a thesis.

Whether point is extracted from incident or incident is supplied to verify point, the two are presented as having an equation-like relationship, with story on one side of the equals sign and point on the other. In this view, the essential nature of an essay story is its compressibility. Put another way, the story stands for the thesis, and in essays in which the thesis is implicit, the story stands alone.

There are two dismal effects of this artificial genre, the classroom narrative essay. First, the classroom narrative essay so fixes students on thesis as label for experience, that there is no possibility of active connection, no sense that the topic at hand is connectable to any other. As a result, their essays circle theses like stone-splashed rings in a pond, finally dissipating, self-contained. However, connection-making – between experience and reading and ideas and news – has been at the heart of the personal essay since its inception with Montaigne.[2] These connections are less logical than linear – than narrative, in fact. This is the realization made by Joan Didion (1979, p. 11):

> We tell ourselves stories in order to live. . . . We interpret what we see, select the most workable of the multiple choices. We live entirely, especially if we are writers, by the imposition of a narrative line upon disparate images, by the 'ideas' with which we have learned to freeze the shifting phantasmagoria which is our actual experience.

More to the point of this chapter is the second consequence of the classroom narrative essay: the obfuscation of real sources of persuasion in personal essays. Elsewhere (Hesse, in press), I have reviewed the conventional wisdom regarding proof through storytelling. It boils down to two tenets: first, that the highest virtue a story in an expository writing class has is to recreate reality so faithfully that readers feel like 'they were there'; second, that when writers assign a meaning to experience faithfully told, that meaning should be stated or statable as a thesis – that the story proves the thesis.

However, my own reading of the personal essay tradition from Addison and Steele, through Lamb, Woolf and Orwell, to Eiseley, Dillard and Lewis Thomas suggests that stories in essays exist less to *prove* points than to *make* points (see Hesse 1986). Shortly, I will show that this distinction is not mere semantic quibbling. But for now let me observe that it is unreasonable to base a judgement of the cognitive difficulty and rhetorical complexity of narrative on faulty textbook precepts.

Unless they follow literary theory, most writing teachers, I suspect, would be surprised to learn how complicated the very idea of narrative has become. At the end of his book, *Recent Theories of Narrative*, Wallace Martin (1986) declares himself unable to say what narrative is. Surely he has in mind a concept more vexed than unchallenged 'common sense' would lead us to believe. Reviewing attempts to define 'story', Thomas Leitch (1986, p. 18) points out that commonly-cited 'distinctive' features like sequence, change, action and closure are all shared by non-narrative works. Even straightforward definitions like Robert Scholes's (1981, p. 205) 'A narration is the symbolic presentation of a sequence of events connected by subject matter and related by time' is vexed by the term 'event'. What counts as event? To recount in detail how something as apparently simple as narrative seems to have become so confused would take more space than is possible here.

However, one definitional issue, the difference between narrative and story, has particular bearing on my argument. While the terms tend to collapse on one another, narrative need not be story any more than a musical composition written in the dorian mode need be a scale. Recognizing the distinction between narrative as a mode and narrative as a form (a familiar structuralist definition – Scholes's – defines stories as narratives with a specific syntactic shape: beginning, middle and end) allows for a more sophisticated view of personal essays.[3] Some essays do, in fact, contain stories, identifiable chunks of text, set pieces whose 'boundaries' are clearly distinguishable. For such *essays with stories* the story often does function as proof or illustration of a point. In addition, there are *stories as essays*, works like George Orwell's 'A Hanging', which consist entirely of the narration of events, a story whose boundaries coexist with the boundaries of the essay it comprises. Less clearly recognized, however, and most important to my argument in this chapter, are *essays as stories*. (Note the distinction I'm making between *stories as essays* and *essays as stories*; the latter do not strictly consist of reported events of 'things that happened' in 'the real world', the relation of experience, for example. Rather, such essays are story-like in their form; they present propositions and report and exposition in a narrative form, this 'causing' that, so that the entire essay has the shape and, as I'll argue later, the persuasive force of story.)

How essays can be conceived as stories is explicable through a structuralist analysis proposed by Meier Sternberg (1978). Theorizing, simply, that stories consisted of action and exposition, Sternberg offered ways to decide which was which in a given text, a task harder than it may sound, since a passage whose *aim* is expositional may itself be narrative. The problem, difficult enough in short stories and in stories as essays (recall my three-part taxonomy, above) is doubly complicated in essays *with* stories, since they have two levels of exposition, one that 'belongs to' the story and one that 'belongs to' the essay. Furthermore, I suggest that in essays *as* stories, 'essay-level' and 'story-level' exposition merge, with the result that the whole essay can be read as story.

Consider George Orwell's 'Shooting an Elephant', in which Orwell intersperses the report of his actions with analysis of them. The opening two paragraphs of the essay contain a combination of apparently story-level

*Story level*

exposition ('I was a police officer in Moulmein in Lower Burma'), apparently essay-level exposition ('I was all for the Burmese and all against their oppressors, the British'), and abstraction ('Feelings like these are the normal by-products of imperialism'). The third paragraph begins with a good story signal, establishing what Sternberg (1978) would call the 'scenic norm' of the story: 'One day something happened which in a roundabout way was enlightening' (Orwell 1961, p. 16). However, instead of the story in the essay beginning here, I suggest it has begun in the first two paragraphs. Orwell's observations about imperialism are part of the narrative sequence. Within the narrative of action, this mixed exposition (of the incident reported, of Orwell's ideas about them) is made part of the storyline.

Consider Orwell's (1961, p. 20) assessment: 'At that age I was not squeamish about killing animals, but I had never shot an elephant and never wanted to'. It explains his actions and therefore seems to lie within the story, but it also explains the realization that forms the point of the essay. The extent to which white men destroy their own freedom is clarified by our knowing that Orwell had never wanted to kill an elephant. All this exposition serves an aesthetic function, that of delay, but it also results in a breakdown of distinctions between the story level and the essay.

Most interesting are those sentences that abstract to interpret what is happening. In 'Shooting an Elephant', these statements have a specified chronological place, since Orwell offers them as thoughts in reaction to specific scenes and events. Now, in a short story, what a narrator thinks has a curious mixed status. Those thoughts are both events in the story and exposition that guides our understanding and interpretation of the action. This is true for essay stories, too, although in them we tend to de-emphasize thought-as-event in favour of thought-as-interpretation.

The most notable piece of abstractive exposition in 'Shooting an Elephant' is the passage in which Orwell (1961, p. 19) claims 'at this moment' to grasp that 'When the white man turns tyrant it is his own freedom that he destroys'. Here is the stuff of essays: an assertion, a proposition, a point. Orwell presents it as a story event, something he realized at that moment, though common sense tells us that the words on the page are hardly his exact ones as he stood there holding the elephant gun. Recalling the dilemma posed in the opening two paragraphs, it is clear that this statement resolves the double tension of his simultaneously hating both the British and the natives. But notice the source of 'proof' for his point. Orwell's narration of one encounter hardly satisfies as evidence for such a universal pronouncement. Instead, we accept the proposition as reasonable because it is a plausible part of the story.

To make a point is to establish a juncture in the line of words that comprises the essay, a place at which propositions can reasonably be stated. Such points are part of the story in the same way that exposition is part of a story.

## Narrative as a *form* of persuasion

It should be clear at this point that narrative in essays plays a more complicated
role in persuasion than simply furnishing sufficient evidence, chunks of proof. In
that traditional view, stories in essays are persuasive when they create for readers
'a clear and detailed picture of what actually happened'. Persuasiveness, therefore, rests in *mimesis*. In this view, rhetorical force derives from a close fit between
words and events 'as they happened', which grants veracity to whatever the writer
may say about those events. The appeal is ethical, in a sense. Readers believe that
writers able convincingly to reproduce reality can be trusted accurately to say
what that reality means. Some theorists, following the nineteenth-century realist
tradition, perceive narrative as 'natural' or 'fundamental', inescapable since we
live in time, in a world of before and after (see, for example, Kermode 1967).
However, persuasion through mimesis should strike even the most naive writing
teacher as inadequate. Textbook advice for the classroom narrative essay usually
tells students to present events in some order other than true chronology, if a
better effect can be gained from doing so. Indeed, one of the most basic analytic
strategies of formalist narrative theorists was to distinguish between a story's
*fabula*, the order in which things 'really happened', and its *sujet*, the order of
presentation that the author gave the story (the clearest explanation of this
method of analysis is Chatman 1978). If 'better effect' dictates occasionally
retelling the story, then artifice rather than mimesis explains the sources of
persuasion.

Other theorists, accordingly, stress the conventional nature of stories. Instead
of being 'natural', stories are human constructs that throughout the centuries
have been reified so that now they seem natural. In this conception, readers only
appear to judge the truth of a story by comparing it to the world as it is. Instead
they compare it to their schemata of stories, the evaluation taking the form 'Does
this piece match story conventions as I know them?' The persuasive force of
narrative is best understood through the lens of narrative as convention, through
Aristotelian, not Platonic, mimesis.

Narrative as such received little attention from the classical rhetoricians.
Aristotle described it primarily as the recital of necessary background facts in
ceremonial and judicial oratory. It is the raw stuff (the 'acts', over which the orator
has no control) to be used in argument (1924 p. 1416b). In addition, he saw
narration as furnishing a vehicle for ethical and emotional appeals (1924
p. 1417a). The *Rhetorica ad Alexandrum* offers some guidelines for presenting
narratives and three methods for arranging narrative in the proem. Cicero
generally took a broader view of narrative as an exposition of events that could, in
addition to stating the case, also serve as a digression to attack someone, make a
comparison, or amuse the audience (I, c. 27, 55). These last are the classical
antecedents of Hugh Blair's belletristic emphases. Richard Whately's popular
*Elements of Rhetoric* pegged narration merely as a possible introductory strategy
(Whately 1845, p. 115) and echoed Aristotle's advice (in the *Rhetoric*, Book II,

c. 20) on using illustrations and fables as proof – inferior, of course, to logical forms like the enthymeme (Whately 1845, pp. 68–70).

I sketch this selective history only to point out that there is little about narrative as persuasion in the classical rhetorical tradition. In pre-twentieth-century terms, personal essays that relied substantially on narrative were decidedly *a*rhetorical.[4] The upshot was that the personal became largely an orphan genre, one susceptible neither to the analysis of classical rhetoric (which would have won its place in composition) nor to the methods of the New Criticism (which would have qualified it for literature). It is clear that the essay was – and continues – to be a victim of our failure to recognize and apply the appropriate theory.

As I remarked at the chapter's outset, that theory lies not in Aristotle's *Rhetorica* but in his *De Poetica*. To make my point quite explicit, if not fully clear: to the extent that essays are emplotted they persuade by appealing to their readers' sense of well-formedness, born in their familiarity with stories, nurtured by their desire for concordance.

Conventional readings of *De Poetica* would have little problem accounting for persuasion in stories in essays. Such readings, by shallowly interpreting *mimesis* as copying the world in words, attribute form in stories to the order that exists in nature. The author, of course, has to decide where the story begins and ends – in fact, must create the sense of an ending – but even this is reconcilable with mimesis in shallow readings of *De Poetica*: the world exists in episodes, events bounded by causality so that the writer of stories is more a finder than a constructor of plots. Those who read mimesis in *De Poetica* in this way have no difficulty smugly chiding Aristotle's ingenuousness. Order exists, they note, because men and women make it exist; it is intertextual, not inherent. The 'realism' of a work is determined not by our comparing it with 'life' but by the dominant conventions of producing 'realistic' texts.

The shortcoming with the conventional reading of *mimesis*, as Paul Ricoeur (1984, p. 34) demonstrates, is its failure to recognize that Aristotle defines mimesis – 'the imitation or representation of action' – in terms of *muthos* – emplotment or 'the organization of the events' (Ricoeur 1984, p. 34). The relationship between imitating and plot-making is circular, with truth determined not by comparing a plot to the world 'out there', as in shallow readings of *De Poetica*, but by comparing it to other texts. As Ricoeur (1984, p. 34) puts it: 'Imitating or representing is a mimetic activity inasmuch as it produces something, namely, the organization of events by emplotment'. The 'test' of mimesis, then, is whether a plot exists. And the test of a plot? The 'combination of the incidents' (Aristotle 1924, p. 1450a), the creation of a beginning, middle and end. Note that Aristotle does not define it in terms of bringing the incidents into some 'shape' provided by nature. The apparently shallow formula 'beginning, middle, and end' is actually far shrewder, since it describes the functioning of the plot in its own terms. As Ricoeur notes, Aristotelian mimesis is not Platonic; in no sense is the author being 'twice removed' from the real.[5]

Why is this reunderstanding of Aristotle so important, especially since it seems to lead to the same point I described earlier, that of narrative as construct and not something 'natural'? It is significant because it creates broader definitions of 'action' and narrative. Instead of action consisting of 'physical events as they may happen in the world' – in other words, what composition textbooks mean by 'narrative' as opposed to 'non-narrative' parts of essays – action might be seen instead as movement and narrative as the creation of plot. We would do well, then, to consider the sense in which essays can be viewed as being emplotted, their propositions as events in the essay as story. When Orwell asserts, 'When the white man turns tyrant it is his own freedom that he destroys', he gives it a place in the essay as story. The stating of the proposition is an event caused, as it were, by prior events.

The reader's perception of causal sequences is crucial to persuasion through emplotment. To say 'this' happened as a result of 'that' is to supply a relationship between the two, to make a judgement. We perceive a state of affairs and wish to explain how it has come to exist, searching backwards, asking in 'digressive' essays, for example, 'How did the writer get *here*?' I propose that we view certain propositions in essays, especially those to which we'd like to grant the status of 'thesis', not as having been proved but as having been caused. This does not necessarily mean that the essayist first settled on a point, then sorted backwards for a series of ideas or events that could be seen as leading up to it. Instead, the *reader* perceives the proposition as having been caused.

At the heart of persuasion in essays, then, is a relationship between writers and readers that pivots on the conventions of storytelling and storyreading they bring to texts. Knoblauch and Brannon (1984, p. 52) have argued that writers simultaneously create the means of knowing and the shape of knowledge. Composition is a process of differentiating in order to synthesize, making assertions ('the verbal expression of relationships'), and connecting them to form larger patterns of meaning (Knoblauch and Brannon 1984, 65–9). Coherence depends on the entailment of assertions, an orderly movement of mind reflected in a sequential interconnection of statements; readers perceive coherence when they perceive the force of a work's entailments (Knoblauch and Brannon 1984, pp. 70–2). An author, therefore, who is able to present something well-formed persuades largely by allowing the reader easily to perceive form. The power arcs between ethical appeal ('Here is someone who is able to form well, so what he says must be true') and the creation of something where there was nothing: 'Here is a constellation. Without a competing version, why should I doubt its existence?' Given the apparent primacy of narrative and story, what more compelling way to reveal form? What more alluring thing than to present story as essay when, as Knoblauch and Brannon (1984, p. 62) put it, 'The coherence of a text conveys a fiction about its certitude', and a story *is* coherence?

Here is a point of convergence between fictional and non-fictional narrative. The 'truth' of history has long been a matter of debate among philosophers of history (see White 1980). Louis Mink (1978, p. 131) notes that our general willingness to view good history as objective truth is simply a cultural predisposition for narrative over other 'primary cognitive instruments' such as theory and metaphor. As 'a primary and irreducible form of human comprehension' (Mink 1978, p. 132), narrative is a means by which order is *constructed* rather than *represented*: 'The cognitive function of narrative form, then, is not just to relate a succession of events but to body forth an ensemble of relationships' (Mink 1978, p. 144). The crucial offshoot is that in historical narrative, *the form claims truth*.

The rhetorical force of personal essays, then, is formal and conventional, not mimetic. Bruner (1986) discusses two cognitive modes. The first, the paradigmatic or logico-scientific, convinces us of truth through formal proof. In works governed by this mode, form is described as the strata of propositions, the relation of parts hierarchically and therefore logically to one another. In such a conception, stories in essays are chunks of 'support' or 'proof' for propositions. Bruner's second mode, the narrative, convinces us of lifelikeness. I would explain this differently. Stories convince not because they are life-like but because they are story-like. The power of narrative in essays comes from assertions offered in a shape that is attractive because it is so familiar. 'Story' is a form of narrative argument in the way that 'syllogism' is of logical.

Argument by narrative draws its power from the reader's involvement in configuring a text. 'Narrativity', a shorthand term for this concept, grows out of a view of narrative as essentially transactional. Thomas Leitch (1986, p. 34) notes that 'narrativity entails three skills':

> the ability to defer one's desire for gratification (so that even if the opening five minutes of a film do not make obvious sense or provide pleasure, we still assume the film will ultimately justify our attention); the ability to supply connections among the material a story presents; and the ability to perceive discursive events as significantly related to the point of a given story or sequence.

The writer controls to a large extent the amount of narrativity necessary to read a given text. If the writer identifies specifically the relation of every aspect of the text to its point, then the reader need exercise only minimal narrativity. The concept of narrativity might well be applied not only to stories as stories but also to essays as stories. Skilled readers of personal essays know that apparent digressiveness can be resolved into purposeful order, that such works 'lead somewhere' through various movements, to a point that makes the leading clear.

Encouraging narrativity in readers involves them in the enterprise of the essay. The result is a rhetorical advantage similar to the one that accrues with such strategies as 'showing, not telling'. Inviting, even forcing, the reader to construct a sense of order in the text makes him or her complicit with the writer. Power comes to writers when they give essays the shape of story because of a fundamental disposition that we have toward stories. The rhetorical value of stories, then, is participatory, not logical. Leitch (1986, p. 199) puts it this way: 'Stories are designed not primarily to provide information but to give their audience a certain kind of experience – the experience of making sense of a world designed precisely to respond to their attempts'.

### The future of a narrative rhetoric

Ricoeur (1985) worries about the 'end' of narrative in the face of such post-modern challenges as those made by Jean-François Lyotard (1984, p. 81), who declares: 'The postmodern would be that which . . . denies itself the solace of good forms.' Ricoeur (1985, p. 28) writes:

> Perhaps, indeed, we are the witnesses – and the artisans of a certain death, that of the art of telling stories, from which proceeds the art of narrating in all its forms. . . . Nothing, therefore, excludes the possibility that the metamorphosis of the plot will encounter somewhere a boundary beyond which we can no longer recognize the formal principle of temporal configuration that makes a story a whole and complete story. And yet . . . and yet. Perhaps, in spite of everything, it is necessary to have confidence in the call for concordance that today still structures the expectations of readers and to believe that new narrative forms, which we do not yet know how to name, are already being born.

The recent rise in popularity of the personal essay, at least in the United States, is due largely to its satisfying a public longing for the kind of concordance through narrative that Ricoeur finds waning in more traditional short prose forms.[6] Post-modern theorists have mounted convincing critiques of the 'healthiness' of a desire for concordance, but it is not my intent here to join this debate. Rather, I simply note that emplotment appears to have found one of its 'new narrative forms' (new since Montaigne, at least) in the personal essay. The essayist casts her or his net widely and consoles the reader with the ability to give disparate material a sense of wholeness. In that consolation lies an argument that the world is not so disjointed as it otherwise seems.

I suggest that personal essays are but the most transparent forms of this more pervasive narrative rhetoric, in which points are made or caused rather than proven deductively. We would do well to begin analysing texts most like personal essays, then move out to the narrative analysis of those apparently dissimilar. Decades after Orwell supposedly killed his elephant, Fallows (1987, p. 20) argues for America's need either to patch up relations with the Soviet Union or to find out 'how to defend ourselves for less'. But this is a point reached only in the last paragraph, and what is captivating is how he gets to it in a piece that begins on a boy scout expedition in 1963, moves through a summary of Gore Vidal's 'requiem for an empire' speech, on to Fallows's (1987, p. 18) criticism of Vidal as racist in his assertion that 'we – the white race – have become the yellow man's burden' and his call for an alliance of all whites, then on to Fallows's recasting Vidal's argument in terms with which he can agree, and ends in the final position I noted above. If we find the essay persuasive at all – and there is certainly much to contest – it is because we perceive a reasonable shape to these rhetorical moves, because the work's final proposition has been so emplotted that the sense of closure we encounter carries the truth of well-formedness.

Writing teachers need to recognize the limitations of textbook depictions of narrative. In particular, we need to recognize that stressing the attachment of 'points' to stories neglects how a narrative may function less as a chunk of evidence than as a form of argument. We should discuss with students how stories can be used not only as bits of proof but also as means of transport, ways of getting readers from place to place, from idea to idea in essays. We should pursue the idea that a work's being formed narratively does not necessarily mean that it consists entirely of action sequences. The essay as story offers a structure to connect all manner of apparently disparate bits of material. Telling students to read for the narrative sequence in their essays often allows them to find places where their writing is static, redundant, or even recursive in an unproductive fashion. Telling them to read for the narrative sequence in published works will show them how to evaluate propositions in terms of their sources of proof: logical or formal. With this I am not arguing that we prize 'inductive' proof over 'deductive' but that we recognize a third mode distinct from these two, the narrative one.

I have attempted to correct, if not complicate, the view of narrative that seems to prevail in writing instruction. I doubt that this corrective will fully offset the political and economic arguments against narrative in undergraduate writing classes, yet I hope it will provide those who wish to join the argument with a richer understanding of the rhetoric of narrative. Convincing proof will most likely come through analyses of 'non-literary' discourse that document narrative persuasion in texts other than personal essays. Bruner (1986, p. 42) has attributed to Robert Heilbroner the statement that 'when forecasts based on economic theory fail, he and his colleagues take to telling stories'. I believe that an analysis of business and political discourse will show that the economists are not alone.

## Notes

1 For an overview of these challenges, see Connors (1987); or Nudelman and Schlosser (1987).

2 Citing the merits of this tradition, Zeiger (1985) has written convincingly for the place of the 'exploratory essay' in the college writing class.

3 Elsewhere (Hesse 1986; in press), I have discussed degrees of narrative in personal essays. Various theorists, most prominently Genette (1972) and Todorov (1977) have proposed story grammars, rules that in various combinations would account for the features of all stories.

4 Perhaps, more precisely, in classical terms essays are governed by almost purely ethical appeals. Early twentieth-century discussions of the essay commonly celebrated the idea of 'voice' or the essayist's projection of self. See, for example, Dawson and Dawson (1932); Dobree (1946); or even Virgina Woolf (1966).

5 Williams's (1948, p. 241) protest about the misinterpretation of the *Poetics* for over two thousand years, illustrates the distinction:

The objective is not to copy nature and never was, but to imitate nature, which involved active invention. . . . It is NOT to hold the mirror up to nature that the artist performs his work. It is to make, out of the imagination, something not at all a copy of nature, but something quite different, a new thing, unlike any thing else in nature, a thing advanced and apart from it.

6  There are various signs of the essay's increased popularity, including the recent publications of single-author essay volumes (by such authors as Lewis Thomas, Annie Dillard, Joan Didion, Gretel Ehrlich, Barry Lopez and Edward Hoaglund); the emergence of 'best-essays' annuals analogous to those that have long appeared for the short story; increased critical attention (at college conferences on composition and communication programmes, at the 'Symposium on the Essay: Redefining a Genre for the Humanities' at Seton Hall University in 1987); and in the publication of two collections of essays on the essay (Anderson, forthcoming; Bertram, forthcoming).

# 11 If it's narrative, why do nothing but generalize?

JOHN DIXON

## An absence in current theories

Reading Imre Salusinszky's (1987) report of his interviews with a range of prominent American literary theorists, I was struck by a family resemblance in their practices. First, when invited to discuss a short poem by Wallace Stevens,* none of them read it aloud. Second, although the poet was narrating and dramatizing an experience, the critics chose largely or entirely to generalize. I doubt whether those two choices arose from a common theoretical commitment; rather, I guess, they are part of a tradition of unanalysed practices that literary theorists still have to penetrate.

Does it make such a difference, you may be asking: after all, such practices are a commonplace of our academic formation. They are indeed. It seems, then, that we had better start by thinking about the ways we actually encounter stories – 'in society' rather than in academe.

Out in the street or the park, say, you come up to me and start telling me the story of this old fellow. One day in March, a scrawny cry from outside seemed like a sound in his mind . . . As I listen, I watch the way you're taking on his role, shaking your head in puzzlement, perhaps, musing as if to yourself. I start imagining him, and how it might be for him. We're both making believe he's there now: you're being him, and I'm an engaged spectator of him in action. And, as you continue, I get a feeling this story might end with a laugh. Yes, you say finally and a bit solemnly: Not Ideas about the Thing, John, but the Thing Itself! You must be having me on, so I lean back and chuckle quietly, still imagining the old chap's goings on.

Stories in the street or the park are socially shared experiences, then; you act out the roles, I watch and listen, and respond, a very close onlooker. You use your

* Readers are referred to Wallace Stevens's poem 'Not Ideas about the Thing but the Thing Itself' in *The Collected Poems of Wallace Stevens* (Faber and Faber, 1955, p. 534) which is discussed in Salusinszky (1987) and in the present essay.

body and voice to make this person real to me, in action; I imaginatively empathize with him and respond to what's happening in the story.

Maybe this tight interweaving of your imagination and mine, this being and watching together, is partly what it's all about? So if, by contrast, some academics habitually refer not to an immediate, shared experience but to a printed text, couldn't that have significant effects? What might tend to happen, for instance, to the reflective conversation that follows a shared story?

## Constructing a 'poem' from a 'text'

In conversation or an interview, we could use the signs on the page to make an imaginative construction – a 'poem' – that would be shaped and expressed through all the communicative systems of the human voice and body. We would treat the text as a 'script'. It is a complex process, now attracting some very interesting theorizing among teachers of English and of reading.

Let us consider a few of the things we would need to attend to in Stevens's text, as we begin that process of construction. Some of the linguistic signs, for instance, indicate discourse choices – generic strategies, you might say – that the writer is adopting as he proceeds.

Thus, Stevens begins with a tacitly introduced *narrator* registering a (minimal) setting before launching into *two key events* (set in the past):

a scrawny cry seemed like a sound . . .
he knew that he heard it . . .

These events, I note, are internal, mental: the narrator is privy to the inner life of the character.

What follows, according to my construction, is a (tacit) transition from narrator to the character's own voice, in the form of *inner speech*, a kind of unspoken deliberation:

the sun was rising at six . . .
it would have been outside . . .
it was not from the vast ventriloquism of sleep . . .

On this construction, then, inner ruminations are being *dramatized* (rather than reported). And the text leaves it open whether this character actually said to himself: 'the sun was rising . . . it would have been outside . . .' or 'the sun is rising . . . it would be outside . . .'. There is an ambiguous possibility, then, of a shift to a dramatic present.

The next line is also ambiguous: 'The sun was coming from outside'. With unmarked stress, it may signal an expectation. With stress on 'was' (or elsewhere) it may indicate that the expected event has already occurred, or is occurring at that moment. Both versions are clearly dramatizing feelings along with thoughts.

Finally, the remaining six lines offer a reflective *comment* on the events, rounding out the more fragmentary ruminations. At least, it seems simplest to read them as an extension of the inner speech.

> That scrawny cry . . . was part of the colossal sun . . . still far away
> It was like/A new knowledge of reality

The strategy of the poetic narrator, then, is to dramatize a shifting flow of thoughts and feelings. We will come back to that.

First, there is a related act of construction to be considered. What is this character doing as he says these things to himself? What speech acts are we to construct? Is he puzzled at first? Surprised? Is he ruminating, as he goes on, a bit wryly, thinking of the papier mâché world he has been in? And towards the end is there a note of triumph, or assurance, or is an edge of irony still present?

What adds to the complexity, of course, is the title: 'Not Ideas about the Thing but the Thing Itself'. With its heavy capitals, it has the generic look and sound of textbook philosophy. This framing suggests an interest in very high-level abstraction: 'Ideas about the Thing', 'the Thing Itself'. The opposition with 'a scrawny cry' couldn't be much sharper, you might say.

Of course, narrative could accommodate even the abstraction of the title. But the two are kept apart. In isolation, the title would read as an invitation to massive generalization, but in this context it seems to be undercut – it could even be mocked.

What does all this imply for the reader's continuing constructions? First, it suggests to me the primacy of the dramatized moment, and the tensions within it. For this reason, the poem I imagine comes nearest to lyric, in Barbara Hardy's (1977) sense, in that the poet 'appears to be creating and discovering feeling', and to invite an apprehension of the complex and dynamic play of feeling. Thus, in my second role, as attentive onlooker, it is fellow-feeling for this character that has the strongest pull for me.

The suspicion that this is a personal poem, in a romantic convention, then suggests a 'construction' of a different kind. If I see 'him' as poet (an old poet at that), producing at last a scrawny cry that sounds like the real thing – not a fading papier mâché scene – that double meaning gives added poignancy, humour and nuance to many of the lines. So I like it and keep that construction going alongside the other. They do not shut out, but complement or extend, each other, it seems to me. The fellow-feeling continues and takes new forms.

But I recognize that this hypothetical construction, reading the character as a type (an elderly man, a poet . . .), is only one of many that are possible. Let us take time to consider why this is so.

## Constructing people as types

Back in the street, as I listened to your story, I knew that each of the people in it could be read as a type. They are professors, say, and we both have our ways of typifying that social role. They are members of certain social institutions – the academy, for instance. They reveal that they belong to ethnic, religious or cultural groups. They have been formed in the mould of a specific social class or nation.

Their gender has probably been a central determinant in that formation. And their family story has archetypical elements.

It is hardly surprising, then, that poetic fictions should present personae who can be read one way or another as representative – in their psychic struggles, their social roles, their group membership, their class and nation, or their gender. So, as we continue reading, all of these potential constructions can be explored, to see what they add or take away. Let us call them 'metaphoric' constructions. None is particularly privileged, it seems to me, unless the text makes it so.

I did try out an obvious one, in this case: 'him' as poet. I also tried 'him' as philosophic man. It didn't seem to work! Hence my current decision to construct the title as undercut, self-mocking. But there are no doubt others that could be productive.

How can we justify treating the 'individual' as 'representative'? I do not think there is a simple answer here. Realism, whether in the Renaissance, in the nineteenth century, or today, clearly opens the way to a deep concern with individual people; in fact each of these eras has taught us to read and structure the 'person' in new ways. Sometimes, following a liberal ideology, the people of these imaginary worlds are seen precisely as the Individual (set against Nature). And maybe there is a touch of the Robinson Crusoe about the character in this Stevens poem, too? But equally, the dominant interest can lie in reading the person as a typical participating member within one or more (conflicting?) social groups.

Either way, many Euro-American plays, novels and lyrics have run towards particularizing the person and the events – moving increasingly into inner as well as outer life. So very important satisfactions in attending to such stories lie in imaginative empathy with a person, in the ebb and flow of sympathy, and in movements of assent and dissent from what goes on, to adapt a phrase of Lionel Knights. I am assuming that as common ground.

Even within this vein of realism, however, it is commonplace that storytellers thematize, say, innocent American young Woman against corrupting European mature Man, and do so quite explicitly. And even where such typifications are raised casually and indirectly, or are left tacit, they may lie very close to the narrative surface. So a prevailing contract within realistic genres seems to invite the reader to construct typifying versions alongside (and in interaction with) the dominant, particularizing generic strategies of the text.

So much is fairly obvious. That leaves us with two questions. First, where does the dominant interest lie in a particular poetic fiction? Second, how does my reading of this fellow as person relate to my further reading of him as representative (as 'poet', for example)? Isn't there going to be some interplay between the two readings? These are the hard questions and I want to postpone considering them till we look at the critical Giants in a moment.

Finally, a rather different point: with certain tellers we come to expect certain things. All storytellers betray more than they know: through their narrators and characters they subconsciously express characteristic values, embodied in characteristic personae. That is an inevitable consequence of their own social and cultural formation. So their work can (and should) be read as social and cultural products, too.

From this point of view, it is unsurprising – nay, typical – when a narrator presents to me a *man* brooding on a *sign* from the *natural world*. In fact, if it is put this way, I can recognize the work as a variation on a long-standing theme. And I can also recognize such themes as shifting components in wider ideological struggles. Struggles about how to shape the family story and act it out, how to shape the social story and actively participate in it . . . ; struggles about who has the chance to tell stories to whom, and for what cultural and social purposes . . . ; struggles about what kinds of reflection on the story are going to count.

## Some questions to critical theorists

Like Brecht's Worker reading History, we can now, I hope, put some questions to Criticism.

To begin in the simplest way, then, what signs are there in the dialogues with Imre Salusinszky that the critics are constructing a poem as they talk, that their bodies and voices are active internally, at least, making that text come alive? For example, do they talk as if they imagined this character doing things, like:

> *registering* some confusion about a sound, maybe . . .
> *feeling surer* what it was . . .
> *recognizing* the source . . .
> *checking back* that the time was right . . .
> *reassuring himself*, becoming more affirmative . . .
> *rejecting* the alternative now – gladly? with relief? with mockery?

and so on, in a kind of progression?

These are the kinds of construction the voice (with facial expressions and gestures) would make if we told the story, dramatizing the inner speech. I am not claiming any privilege for these particular constructions; all I am asking is whether there are any signs that 'speech acts' such as these are imaginatively present?

The answer is a bit of a surprise. So far as I can see, only one critic explicitly refers to what the character is doing. He is musing at this point, says Northrop Frye, quoting the line: 'It would have been outside'. But that is all.

We can read this hole in the evidence in two ways, at this point. Either the progressive shifts in speech act did not seem sufficiently central to be worth making explicit, or they were not being realized and attended to. Let us leave the issue open.

How about the man's feelings, as this progression occurred? Here the evidence for imaginative shaping is much fuller, though significantly constrained. Let us start with Harold Bloom. 'It is an extremely genial and self-celebratory poem' is his construction; 'an authentic and heartening revision of "The Snow Man" . . .

It is a poem of superb self-recovery, and . . . of having healed one's own reductiveness, of having dispelled the "Mrs Alfred Uraguay" in oneself.'

We can make some allowance here for a certain rhetorical style of conversation. What is interesting are the generic choices:

It is a —— poem
It is a poem of ——
    a poem of having —— ed

The impulse, it seems to me, is to categorize, and to offer a single, unifying category. What is more, that category is treated as if it is reported in the poem (as a previous event), not dramatically enacted (within the poem).

This is very strange. Obviously, I can imagine places where the voice may become, as he says, genial, even celebratory. Yes, but is this the only feeling it has to express? That is my first problem. The second is that, for me, constructing the poem means enacting shifts in feeling. Surely that ought to be common ground? And finally, does the poem necessarily end up with something simple and unified, so far as feelings are concerned? I'd have thought that was a question worth considering, at least.

Frank Kermode, who follows later in the series, had a chance to read the transcript of Bloom's interview. What does he have to say? 'I think Bloom said in his interview that it was a self-celebrating poem: that's right.' 'This one ends like waking up on a beautiful summer morning. In that sense it is a happy poem . . . not Sophoclean, but just having a sort of Santayanan contentment . . .'.

Again, the generic conventions are accepted (It is a —— poem; it has a sort of ——), and, in keeping with this, Bloom's unifying category is endorsed. However, there is just a hint of a change:

This one ends like waking up . . .

Something that ends —— inevitably begins differently; but the shifts are not pursued – possibly because (by accident) the text was not available, possibly because the main generic strategy was too engrained?

However, this projection onto 'the poem' of a unified, idealized mood of happiness, contentment, and genial self-celebration was not to last. The next critic, Edward Said, started with a strong feeling of incongruity,

> I mean the incongruity of the 'scrawny cry' and 'Not Ideas about the Thing but the Thing Itself'. That kind of Platonic or classically metaphysical statement, and then this poem which slowly unfolds and in the end gives you the 'scrawny cry' in a context that is obviously taken straight out of the first chorus in Haydn's 'The Creation'. 'Let there be light!': and then instead of a great C-major chord you get this little toot. It's a fantastically funny poem . . . It's a carnival poem; but . . .

This bears thinking about. When things are incongruous – and they do seem to be so in 'Not Ideas' – the feelings they give rise to are unlikely to be single and unified, we might think. Things that are solemn, ceremonial, awe-inspiring, one moment, say, and scrawny, ordinary, and fallible the next, are quite likely to leave us with mixed feelings, surely?

Turning back to Said, I must say that, whether you find the Haydn obviously present or not, the idea of a scrawny cry being a chorister whose C preceded the choir (the choral rings surrounding a colossal sun!) has got to be funny.

Now laughing is not incompatible, by any means, with feeling genial or content. But it suggests a shift in the mood. A relaxation, an unbending – a bit of daftness – something less composed than philosophic contentment, for instance. If it happens in the middle of self-celebration, well, a hint of mockery in your voice certainly takes off any edge of self-satisfaction or self-congratulation, too.

However, having made his point, Said also follows the prevailing generic strategy: 'It's a —— poem'. Again there's only one mood in the poem. He does not turn back to explore the way this poem 'slowly unfolds', as he put it. He does not even consider the incongruity he pointed to in the opening.

At this point in the interviews, then, Salusinszky and the remaining critics faced a serious conflict as they read the transcripts of earlier conversations. Fantastic fun, genial self-celebration – or what? What feelings were they going to enact as they read? To my surprise, the remaining critics have next to nothing to say about this crucial difference, for or against, and Salusinszky says nothing either. I find that puzzling.

How about this divergence of interpretation, then? What is academic 'theory' doing about something so radical? Apparently nothing; the fundamental attitudes and feelings of the poem each of us is creating are not an explicit issue.

And how is that possible? Basically, I believe, because the generic choice is to generalize, not to narrate. Narrative could hardly fail to incorporate feelings and speech acts within its structures; in generalized discussion and argument they can too easily be excluded.

## A tacit focus of critical theorists

This blind spot – blind arc? – doesn't come about through lack of application or intelligence, though. Manifestly, the critics' eyes are elsewhere.

Not surprisingly, being academics some of them are pulled up sharp by the abstract title: 'I suppose I'm really looking for, in this case, a poem which illustrates the title', Frye begins: 'the fact that, when you're dealing with ideas about a thing, you're dealing with statements that have a tendency to become self-enclosed . . . what he's after is a "new knowledge of reality", where you get past the whole inside/outside tail-chasing'.

The title, then, becomes an invitation to philosophize – and in so doing to feel you're joining the poet in a certain kind of quest. This leads pretty inevitably to a metaphoric reading at a high level of abstraction (which, as it happens, Frye does not pursue; nor does anyone else, as a matter of fact). Hillis Miller is baffled by the title ('The poem doesn't give you any support'). Frank Lentricchia sees it as a dangerous invitation to banalities of modernist criticism. Geoffrey Hartman rejects this whole line of interpretation: '"A new knowledge of reality" is a throwaway line; it's a conclusion that says "Something has to be concluded" . . .'. Said is more trenchant still: 'to see in it some metaphysical parable is impossible'.

The apparent invitation to philosophize, then, looks to be a kind of diversion. But what other metaphoric readings was the poem open to? For several of these critics there was a clear alternative. This was first announced (with passionate force) by Bloom:

> What's left [to an aged poet] is to make the next poem possible, which is what is always left; to rally what remains, in the grand Miltonic-Satanic tradition; to rouse up one's fallen forces. What he's doing here is fundamentally what he does, say, in the very great piece, 'An Ordinary Evening in New Haven': it is to vary again his characteristic themes, it is to practise, it is to rehearse again an overcoming of the perpetual crisis that will come again . . . This poem is a 'crisis-poem' because, to use an Emersonian term for it, power resides in the shooting of the gap, in the crossing to an aim; power exists in the moment of transition; it, too, records the power which is gain and loss, loss and gain, in a moment of transition. . . .

Talking in this heady way certainly takes us up into the stratosphere. Power, gain and loss in a moment of transition: that's all a meta-comment, I take it, on a metaphoric reading that was left to Imre and us to construct. If so, what we have to search for is (metaphorically) conveyed as:

> rousing up one's forces . . .
> overcoming the crisis . . .
> shooting the gap . . .
> crossing to an aim . . .

I can respond to the epic tone; it is practically creating a prose poem in its own right. But I find it hard to connect that Miltonic-Satanic fervour with this old fellow waking, still uncertain whether or not that scrawny cry came from outside. Sure, the cry is him too, a scrawny self – and that is all that is left? – recovering its voice, prompting his imagination, promising and perhaps renewing his access to things . . . But let us take Bloom's [transformed] verbs seriously: rousing, overcoming, shooting, crossing to an aim – don't these make the old man out to be far too active an agent?

Part of the trouble, I am sure, is Bloom's generic strategy. Once again, I notice, he goes for a single category: 'this poem is a —— poem'. It is true that this time he shifts into nouns with verbal force – an overcoming, the shooting of the gap, the crossing to an aim. But even here, is he not typifying the experience of the poem as a *single event* – with each noun group slightly extending or reshaping the sense of 'crisis'?

The underlying strategy – conscious or not – is to abstract and to summarize, then. There is nothing wrong with that in itself, I take it, providing there is also room to move on to something more dynamic and particular: to treat the speech acts as some kind of progression, the dramatized attitudes as various, the character's stance to the events as possibly ambiguous, and not necessarily resolved . . .

How does this compare with the other critics who seem to be broadly in sympathy with this kind of thematic reading? I want to begin by drawing various fragments together. Thus, Hartman, after first noticing that 'earliest ending', continues: 'Then I see it as a threshold phrase, and think about the threshold feeling, and am reminded that it is an old age poem.' Thus Hillis Miller asserts 'this is a poem about the appearance of something out of hiddenness, out of occultation: the sun; the cry; spring; the earliest ending of winter; and the poet waking up out of sleep, coming into consciousness'. The manoeuvre of this poem, thinks Lentricchia, is to suggest that 'one is on the verge of a stunned reception, a breakthrough-moment in which something has finally been cracked. It's a moment in which language ceases to suffice – though, of course, he's manipulating language to do this. What he wants to give is the sense of an awe-full reception: an intransitive, ecstatic moment of fullness.' We are expecting, Said indicates, a great C-major chord for The Creation – 'Let there be light!'. Or in Hillis Miller's version: 'the cry that has become all these other things . . . is a new knowledge of reality just at the threshold moment before the sun rises.'

There are exciting possibilities – and, assembled in this way, they give the lie, I would have thought, to any simple characterization of the poem! I will just select a few to highlight and dwell on:

> the threshold feeling . . .
> out of occultation . . .
> coming into consciousness . . .
> the sense of an awe-full reception . . .
> the cry that has become all these other things . . .
> a moment in which language ceases to suffice . . .

These have the advantage for me of being much less abstracted than Bloom, much closer in contact with text and poem. It is true that nouns are still prominent: 'threshold', 'occultation', 'reception'. And each critic favours a single one, rather than a plurality. All the same, taken as a set, they translate more readily into a range of mental activities – which is what this particular metaphoric version is about, I suppose:

> emerging out of an obscured, self-enclosed, fabricated existence . . .
> feeling yourself on the edge, by a boundary, about to cross . . .
> called and responding with active attention . . .
> expecting, knowing the immense potential it might signify . . .
> awaiting (and imagining) a still distant power . . .
> feeling what words won't express . . .

Following these cues as I am trying to do, I have constructed this situation in a more general form. In doing so, I realize that in this form or scheme it might draw together and illumine a wider range of experiences. So, taken as a group, the critics have helped me create a rewarding, though partial, reading of the text.

Why partial? Because it leaves out any fun or wryness! Why does Hillis Miller want to get away from the scrawny cry – to transform it into a 'pitch pipe'? Isn't 'coming into consciousness' too simple? What fullness of reception comes from something 'still far away'? Can you be sure you've 'cracked' it? And most important of all, what has become of those amazing incongruities?

That a scrawny cry should signal the possibility of coming into touch with experience again, that is one thing. But such a grotesque minor cue for such an apocalyptic happening? What are these major theorists making of this kind of question? Very little most of the time, it seems to me.

In part, it is true, answers to such questions are not to be found in theory, but on the street. You want to see the representative side of this old man? Then watch the old fellows over there, or in the park. Scrawny? I'll say. Listen to them cackling – and having visions. It's not all easy, rallying their forces.

Yet there *are* big questions for theory. Only one critic, Barbara Johnson, asked herself: 'Why is this told as a story . . . ?' That kind of interest in discourse might well throw new light on how we each construct a poem, on our conversations in the street, and on the generic choices critics like these (unconsciously?) are making.

By way of conclusion, then, let's add some more questions of our own:

- What happens to narrative if you respond mainly or exclusively with summary generalizations?
- What happens to the .ynamic of narrative if you transform it into a unified category or theme?
- What happens to your typifying metaphor if you do not bring it back into relation with particularized narrative events?
- What happens if you do not acknowledge and theorize the construction of speech acts, attitudes or feelings from textual signs?
- Why did the specific writer/speaker make the generic choices she or he did, and what variety of choices might they open the way to in our responses, if we continued the conversation in the street?
- And last, what about the choice of generic strategies when we shift to discussion and argument, as I have done, especially in the second half?

Then let us finish by picking up Wallace Stevens and reading the poem again (aloud).

## Acknowledgements

Many thanks to Molly Dixon for joining in a series of shared readings of the text and discussing our mutual constructions from it. There is also a long-term debt to Barbara Hardy, for her ideas on lyric and imagination; to Louise Rosenblatt for her distinction between 'text' and 'poem'; and to Les Stratta for his share in our joint discoveries about traditional generic strategies in English Literature – and the dead-ends they often lead students into.

# References and bibliography

Abrahams, R. (1972), 'Joking: the Training of the Man of Words in Talking Broad' in T. Kochman (ed.), *Rappin' and Stylin' Out*, Champaign: University of Illinois Press.

Anderson, C. (ed.) (forthcoming), *Literary Nonfiction*, Carbondale: Southern Illinois University Press.

Aristotle (1924), *Rhetorica, De Rhetorica Ad Alexandrum, De Poetica* in *Works*, vol. 11, Oxford: Oxford University Press.

Austin, J. (1962), *How to Do Things with Words*, Oxford: Oxford University Press.

Bertram, A. J. (ed.) (forthcoming), *Essays on the Essay*, Athens, Georgia: University of Georgia Press.

Birch, D. and O'Toole, M. (eds) (1988), *Functions of Style*, London: Frances Pinter.

Britton, J., Burgess, T., Martin, N., McLeod, A. and Rosen, H. (1975), *The Development of Writing Abilities (11–18)*, London: Macmillan.

Brown, H. and Cambourne, B. L. (1987), *Read and Retell*, Sydney: Methuen.

Bruner, J. (1986), *Actual Minds, Possible Worlds*, Cambridge: Harvard University Press.

Cambourne, B. L. and Turbill, J. B. (1988), 'From Guinea Pigs to Co-Researchers': papers presented at Pre-Conference Institute, World Reading Conference, Surfers' Paradise, Queensland, Australia.

Chatman, S. (1978), *Story and Discourse: Narrative Structure in Fiction and Film*, Ithaca, NY: Cornell University Press.

Christie, F. (1985a), 'Curriculum Genres: Towards a Description of the Construction of Knowledge in Schools', Working Conference on Interaction of Spoken and Written Language, University of New England, NSW, Australia.

Christie, F. (1985b), 'Curriculum genre and schematic structure of classroom discourse' in R. Hasan (ed.), *Discourse on Discourse*, Applied Linguistics Association of Australia, Occasional Papers, no. 7.

Cicero (1949), *De Inventione* (trans. H. M. Hubbell), Cambridge, MA: Harvard University Press.

Clarke, S. (1984), 'An Area of Neglect', *English in Education*, vol. 18, no. 2, pp. 67–73.

Connors, R. J. (1987), 'Personal Writing Assignments', *College Composition and Communication*, vol. 38, pp. 166–83.

Davies, F. and Greene, T. (1984), *Reading for Learning in the Sciences*, Edinburgh: Oliver and Boyd.

Dawson, W. J. and Dawson, C. W. (1932), *The Great English Essayists*, New York: H. W. Wilson.

DES (1988), *English for Ages 5–11* (proposals of the Secretary of State for Education and Science and the Secretary of State for Wales), London: HMSO.

Didion, J. (1979), *The White Album*, New York: Simon and Schuster.

Dixon, J. (1987), 'The Question of Genres' in I. Reid, (ed.), *The Place of Genre in Learning*, Deakin University, Geelong: Centre for Studies in Literary Education.

Dixon, J. and Brown, J. (1984), *Responses to Literature: What is Being Assessed?*, Sheffield: SCDC/NATE.

Dixon, J. and Freedman, A. (1988), *Levels of Abstracting: Invitation to a Dialogue*, Ottawa: Carleton University Occasional Papers.

Dixon, J. and Stratta, L. (1982a), 'Argument: What Does it Mean to Teachers of English?', *English in Education*, vol. 16, pp. 28–39.

Dixon, J. and Stratta, L. (1982b), *Teaching and Assessing Argument*, Discussion Booklet 2: a report on the 1981 CEE English cross-moderation exercise, Southampton: Southern Regional Examinations Board.

Dixon, J. and Stratta, L. (1986), *Writing Narrative – and Beyond*, Canadian Council of Teachers of English.

Dobree, B. (1946), *English Essayists*, London: Collins.

Fallows, J. (1987), 'The White Peril', *The Atlantic*, no. 259 (May), pp. 18–20.

Fox, C. (1988), 'Poppies Will Make Them Grant' in M. Meek and C. Mills (eds), *Language and Literacy in the Primary School*, Basingstoke: Falmer Press.

Fox, C. (1989), 'Children Thinking through Story', *English in Education*, vol. 23, no. 2 (Summer).

Franklin, B. (1964), *The Autobiography of Benjamin Franklin* (ed. L. W. Labaree *et al.*), New Haven, CT: Yale University Press.

Freedman, A. (1987), 'Development in Story Writing', *Applied Psycholinguistics*, vol. 8, pp. 153–69.

Freedman, A. (forthcoming), 'Learning to Write Again', Carleton Papers in Applied Language Study.

Freedman, A. and Pringle, I. (1979), 'The Carleton Writing Project, Part 1: The Writing Abilities of a Selected Sample of Grade 7 and 8 Students', Report prepared for the Carleton Board of Education, 133 Greenbank Road, Nepean, Ontario.

Freedman, A. and Pringle, I. (eds) (1980), *Reinventing the Rhetorical Tradition*, Conway, AR: L & S Books, for CCTE.

Freedman, A. and Pringle, I. (1984), 'Why Students Can't Write Arguments', *English in Education*, vol. 18, no. 2, pp. 73–84.

Frowe, I. (1986), 'Recognising Bias', *English in Education*, vol. 20, no. 2 (Summer).

Geekie, P. and Keeble, P. (1987), 'With a Little Help from My Friends . . .', paper presented at XIVth Australian Reading Conference, Sydney.

Genette, G. (1972), *Narrative Discourse*, Oxford: Basil Blackwell.

Graves, D. (1983), *Writing: Teachers and Children at Work*, London and Exeter, NH: Heinemann Educational Books.

Hardcastle, J. (1985), 'Classrooms as Sites for Cultural Making', *English in Education*, vol. 19, no. 3, pp. 8–22.

Hardy, B. (1966), 'The Advantage of Poetry', *NATE Bulletin* (Spring).

Hardy, B. (1977), *The Advantage of Lyric: Essays on Feeling in Poetry*, London: Athlone Press.

Hasan, R. (ed.) (1985), *Discourse on Discourse: Workshop Report from the Macquarie Workshop on Discourse Analysis*, Applied Linguistics Association of Australia, Occasional Papers no. 7.

Hesse, D. (1986), 'The story in the essay', PhD thesis, University of Iowa.

Hesse, D. (in press), 'Stories in Essays, Essays as Stories' in C. Anderson (ed.), *Literary Nonfiction*, Carbondale: Southern Illinois University Press.

Hodge, R. I. V. and Kress, G. R. (1988), *Social Semiotics*, Oxford: Polity Press.

Horner, S. (ed.) (1983), *Best Laid Plans*, York: Longman.

Kermode, F. (1967), *The Sense of an Ending*, New York: Oxford University Press.

Kinneavy, J. (1971), *A Theory of Discourse*, Englewood Cliffs, NJ: Prentice Hall.

Kinneavy, J. (1980), 'A Pluralistic Synthesis of Four Contemporary Models for Teaching Composition' in A. Freedman and I. Pringle (eds), *Reinventing the Rhetorical Tradition*, Conway, AR: L & S Books, for CCTE.

Kinneavy, J., McCleary, W. and Nakadate, N. (1985), *Writing in the Liberal Arts Tradition: A Rhetoric with Readings*, New York: Harper and Row.

Knoblauch, C. H. and Brannon, L. (1984), *Rhetorical Traditions and the Teaching of Writing*, Upper Montclair, NJ: Boynton/Cook.

Kress, G. R. (1982), *Learning to Write*, London: Routledge & Kegan Paul.

Kress, G. R. (1985), 'Sociolinguistic Development and the Mature Language User' in G. Wells and J. Nicholls (eds), *Language and Learning*, Lewes: Falmer Press.

Kress, G. R. (1986a), 'Interrelations of reading and writing' in A. Wilkinson (ed.), *The Writing of Writing*, Milton Keynes: Open University Press, pp. 198–214.

Kress, G. R. (1986b), 'Reading, Writing and Power' in C. Painter and J. R. Martin (eds), *Writing to Mean*, Applied Linguistics Association of Australia, Occasional Papers no. 9.

Kress, G. R. (1987), 'Genre in a Social Theory of Language' in I. Reid (ed.), *The Place of Genre in Learning*, Deakin University, Geelong: Centre for Studies in Literary Education.

Kress, G. R. (1988), *Linguistic Processes in Sociocultural Practice*, Geelong/Oxford: Deakin University Press/Oxford University Press.

Kress, G. R. (1989), *Writing as Social Practice*, London: Routledge.

Kress, G. R. and Threadgold, T. (1988), 'Towards a Social Theory of Genre', *Southern Review*, vol. 21, no. 3, pp. 215–43.

Leitch, Thomas M. (1986), *What Stories Are: Narrative Theory and Interpretation*, University Park: Pennsylvania State University Press.

Lightfoot, M. and Martin, N. (eds) (1988), *The Word for Teaching Is Learning*, London: Heinemann Educational/Portsmouth, NH: Boynton/Cook.

Lyotard, J.-F. (1984), *The Postmodern Condition: A Report on Knowledge*, Minneapolis: University of Minnesota Press.

Marriott, J. W. (1923), *Exercises in Thinking and Expression*, London: Harrap.

Martin, J. R. (1984), 'Language, Register, Genre' in *Language Studies: Children Writing – A Reader*, Geelong: Deakin University Press.

Martin, J. R. (1985), *Factual Writing: Exploring and Challenging Social Reality*, Geelong: Deakin University Press.

Martin, J. R. and Rothery, J. (1981a), *Writing Project Report No. 1*, Sydney University Linguistics Department.

Martin, J. R. and Rothery, J. (1981b), 'The Ontogenesis of written genres', Sydney University Linguistics Department, Working Papers in Linguistics no. 2.

Martin, N. (1986), 'Research Currents: What Writers! What Readers! What Thinkers!', *Language Arts*, vol. 63, pp. 170–6.

Martin, W. (1986), *Recent Theories of Narrative*, Ithaca, NY: Cornell University Press.

Medway, P. (1986), 'What Gets Written About' in A. Wilkinson (ed.), *The Writing of Writing*, Milton Keynes: Open University Press.

Meek, M. (1984), 'Speaking of shifters' in M. Meek and J. Miller (eds), *Changing English*, London: Institute of Education.

Mink, L. O. (1978), 'Narrative Form as a Cognitive Instrument' in R. Canary and H. Kozicki (eds), *The Writing of History: Literary Form and Historical Understanding*, Madison: University of Wisconsin Press.

Moffett, J. (1968), *Teaching the Universe of Discourse*, Boston: Houghton Mifflin.

Nudelman, J. and Schlosser, A. H. (1987), 'Experiential vs. Expository: Is Peaceful Coexistence Really Possible?' in T. Enos (ed.), *A Sourcebook for Basic Writing Teachers*, New York: Random House, pp. 497–506.

Orwell, G. (1961), 'Shooting an Elephant' in *Collected Essays*, London: Secker and Warburg.

Painter, C. and Martin, J. R. (eds) (1986), *Writing to Mean: Teaching Genres across the Curriculum*, Applied Linguistics Association of Australia, Occasional Papers no. 9.

Pratt, M. L. (1977), *Toward a Speech Act Theory of Literary Discourse*, Bloomington: Indiana University Press.

Prince, G. (1982), *Narratology: the Form and Functioning of Narrative*, Berlin: Mouton.

Pringle, I. and Freedman, A. (1984), 'The Scarborough Writing Assessment Project: An Analysis of In-class and Out-of-class Expository Writing by a Selected Sample of Students in Grade 8 and Grade 12', report prepared for the Scarborough Board of Education, Toronto, Ontario.

Pringle, I. and Freedman, A. (1985), *A Comparative Study of Writing Abilities in two Modes at the Grades 5, 8 and 12 Levels*, Toronto: Ontario Ministry of Education.

Protherough, R. (1987), 'The Stories that Readers Tell' in B. Corcoran and E. Evans (eds), *Readers, Texts, Teachers*, Milton Keynes: Open University Press.

Raban, J. (1987a), 'The Journey and the Book' in *For Love and Money*, London: Collins Harvill.

Raban, J. (1987b), 'Living in London', in *For Love and Money*, London: Collins Harvill.

Raban, J. (1988), *Soft City*, London: Collins Harvill.

Reid, I. (ed.) (1987), *The Place of Genre in Learning: current debates*, Deakin University, Geelong: Centre for Studies in Literary Education.

Reising, R. J. (1986), *The Unusable Past: Theory and the Study of American Literature*, London: Methuen.

Ricoeur, P. (1984), *Time and Narrative*, vol. 1, Chicago: University of Chicago Press.

Ricoeur, P. (1985), *Time and Narrative*, vol. 2, Chicago: University of Chicago Press.

Ricoeur, P. (1988), *Time and Narrative*, vol. 3, Chicago: University of Chicago Press.

Rose, M. (1983), 'Remedial Writing Courses: A Critique and a Proposal', *College English*, vol. 45, pp. 109–28.

Rosen, H. (1958) in consultation with Nancy Martin, 'What Shall I Set?', *The Use of English*, vol. 10, no. 2, pp. 90–7.

Rosen, H. (1984), *Stories and Meanings*, Sheffield: NATE.

Rosen, H. (1985), 'The Autobiographical Impulse', paper prepared for HEH Institute, Georgetown University, Washington, DC.

Rosen, H. (1986), 'The Importance of Story', *Language Arts*, vol. 63, no. 3 (March).

Rosen, H. (1988a), 'The Irrepressible Genre' in M. Maclure *et al.* (eds), *Oracy Matters*, Milton Keynes: Open University Press.

Rosen, H. (1988b), 'Stories of Stories: footnotes on sly gossipy practices' in M. Lightfoot and N. Martin (eds), *The Word for Teaching Is Learning*, London: Heinemann Educational/Portsmouth, NH, Boynton/Cook.

Rosenblatt, L. (1978), *The Reader, the Text, the Poem*, Carbondale: Southern Illinois University Press.

Rumelhart, D. (1977), 'Understanding and Summarising Brief Stories' in D. La Berget (ed.), *Basic Processes in Reading*, Hillsdale, NJ: Lawrence Erlbaum Associates.

Said, E. (1984), *The World, the Text and the Critic*, London: Faber.

Salusinszky, Imre (1987), *Criticism in Society*, London: Methuen.

Scholes, R. E. (1981), 'Language, Narrative and Anti-Narrative', *Critical Inquiry*, vol. 7.

Scholes, R. E. (1982), 'Narrativity in Film and Fiction' in *Semiotics and Interpretation*, New Haven, CT: Yale University Press.

Searle, J. (1969), *Speech Acts: An Essay in the Philosophy of Language*, Cambridge: Cambridge University Press.

Searle, J. (1979), *Expression and Meaning: Studies in the Theory of Speech Acts*, Cambridge: Cambridge University Press.

Sternberg, M. (1978), *Expositional Modes and Temporal Ordering in Fiction*, Baltimore, MD: Johns Hopkins University Press.

Stevens, F. (1960), *The Living Tradition: the Social and Educational Assumptions of the Grammar School*, London: Hutchinson.

Summerfield, J. and Summerfield, G. (1986), *Texts and Contexts*, New York: Random House.

Thorndyke, P. and Yekovitch, F. (1980), 'A Critique of Schemata as a Theory of Human Story Memory', *Poetics*, vol. 9.

Threadgold, T. *et al.* (eds) (1986), *Semiotics – Ideology – Language*, Sydney: SASSC.

Threadgold, T. (1987), 'The Semiotics of Halliday, Voloshinov and Eco', *American Journal of Semiotics*, vol. 4, no. 2.

Threadgold, T. (1988a), 'The genre debate: review of Ian Reid (ed.) *The Place of Genre in Learning*', *Southern Review*, vol. 23, no. 3, pp. 315–30.

Threadgold, T. (1988b), 'Stories of Race and Gender: An Unbounded Discourse' in D. Birch and M. O'Toole (eds), *Functions of Style*, London: Frances Pinter.

Todorov, T. (1977), *The Poetics of Prose*, trans. Richard Howard, Ithaca, NY: Ithaca University Press.

Tompkins, J. (1981), 'Sentimental Power: Uncle Tom's Cabin and the Politics of Literary History', *Glyph*, vol. 8, pp. 79–103.

Vygotsky, L. (1962), *Thought and Language*, Cambridge, MA: MIT Press.

Vygotsky, L. (1978), *Mind in Society: the Development of Higher Psychological Processes*, Cambridge, MA: Harvard University Press.

Walkerdine, V. (1982), 'A Psychosemiotic Approach to Abstract Thought' in M. Beveridge (ed.), *Children Thinking through Language*, London: Edward Arnold.

Wells, G. and Nicholls, J. (eds) (1985), *Language and Learning: An Interactional Perspective*, Lewes: Falmer Press.

Whately, R. (1845), *Elements of Rhetoric*, Boston: James Munroe.

White, H. (1980), 'The value of narrativity in the representation of reality', *Critical Inquiry*, vol. 7, pp. 5–27.

Wilkinson, A. *et al.* (1980), *Assessing Language Development*, Oxford: Oxford University Press.

Wilkinson, A. (ed.) (1986), *The Writing of Writing*, Milton Keynes: Open University Press.

Williams, J. (1984), 'Cognitive Development, Critical Thinking and the Teaching of Writing', paper presented at the Conference of Writing, Meaning and Higher Order Reasoning, Chicago, Illinois.

Williams, W. C. (1948), *Autobiography*, New York: MacGibbon and Kee.

Williams-Ellis, A. (ed.) (1959), *Grimm's Fairy Tales*, Glasgow: Blackie.

Woolf, V. (1966), 'The Modern Essay' in *Collected Essays*, vol. 2, London: Hogarth Press, pp. 41–50.

Zeiger, W. (1985), 'The Exploratory Essay: Enfranchising the Spirit of Inquiry in College Composition', *College English*, vol. 47, pp. 454–66.

# Index